The Journey Home to My Heart

The Journey Home to My Heart

Ullis Karlsson,
Ullis Karlsson Publishing

Ullis Karlsson Publishing, Fredrikslundsvägen 8, 168 34 Bromma, Sweden
www.ulliskarlsson.com

Photos Frontcover/backcover: Anders Lindqvist
First Edition: June 2019
ISBN: 978-91-519-1736-8
Printed in Spauda AB, Lithuania

The Journey Home to My Heart

BY ULLIS KARLSSON

Edited by Joe St Clair

Design by Dorian Çipi

Acknowledgments

This book is dedicated to my beloved children, Elliot and Livia. Thank you for unknowingly saving my life. To me, you were like lighthouses, beaming your love and light, guiding me through the darkness back into life. Thank you for being in my life and for giving it meaning. You are my greatest teachers in life.

Thank you, to my Mother and my Father, who always did your very best. I am so grateful to you, for giving me this gift called life. Thank you for your love and support.

Thank you, Dennis Larsson, for your love, patience and companionship.

Thank you to all my loving, supportive

friends, for believing in me when I didn't believe in myself.

Thank you, Kicki Pallin, my book coach, for your energy, time, and valuable feedback and making this book come true.

Thank you, to all the people I met along the way who somehow contributed in making my rollercoaster life so meaningful and valuable.

Thank you, dear reader, for taking some of your valuable time to read this book. I hope you find it inspiring, and if so, please pass it on to someone who you think could benefit from reading it as well.

And lastly, thank you Universe - and thank you, life!

With Love and Light,
Ullis Karlsson

8

Life influences us from the very first years of our existence.

I might look innocent, but the foundation of my future illness was already starting to manifest. Being an empath meant taking in everything and not being able to distinguish between my own and other people's energies…

Ullis - 1 year old

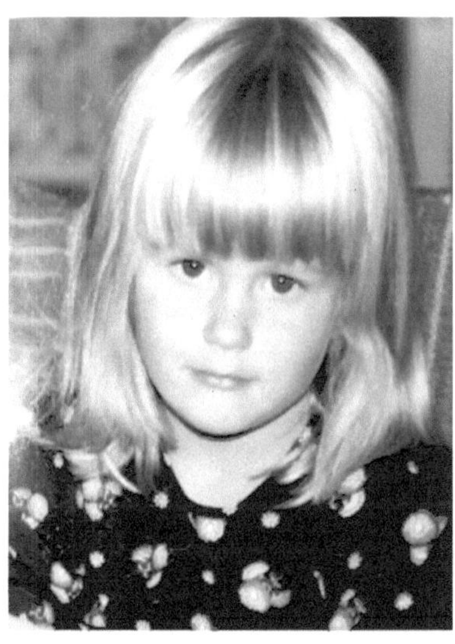

Ullis - 4 years old

PART
I

2:47 AM

I am being completely thrown but I don't know at which time and in which order. I lost count a very long time ago. Once again, I am being thrown, with a silent scream, out of a nightmare which is so terribly scary and yet so extremely familiar. My heart is pumping and pounding in my chest and it feels like it is bursting. It feels like my heart is going to explode into a thousand razor-sharp pieces.

My jaws are clenched so tightly together that I can feel the pain in the jaws every time I try to open them. My tongue is glued to my palate and there is a sharp metallic taste of blood in my mouth. It makes me feel sick and it also feels like the blood is being intensely pumped out from my vessels into my whole body. And I'm scared to death. Just as I always am after this dream. This incredibly scary but, at the same time, very familiar dream.

I am covered in my own sweat. My body is completely wet. My hair is stuck; glued to the temples and to the neck. My breath is jerky and interrupted. I breathe in total panic. I am gulping for air. But I can't seem to get any air at all. It feels like I'm going to die. It is pitch black in the room and, for a short moment, I am completely disoriented. Confused. The only thing I can see when my eyes begin to focus is the red numbers on a digital alarm clock showing 2:47 AM.

Where am I?

My shaking hands are fumbling, exploring and grabbing for something in the darkness and touching the sweat-damp and wrinkled sheets. And, as I continue to explore the darkness around me with my hands, I can feel my husband's warm body lying close. Through my own strong heartbeats that echo in my ears, I can hear his soft sniffing. I am lying in my bed, next to my husband.

The violent images of yet another nightmare continue to play in my head and burn on the retina. Memorable, detailed and unspeakably horrible memories, where I see myself being murdered every night. It's just the environment in which I get murdered that changes. Sometimes it is in the bathtub, sometimes it is in the bed, sometimes it is outdoors. Slaughtered, again and again. Tortured. And there is blood everywhere. My blood. I am bathing in my own blood and still I continue to try to protect myself from the stabbing knife that comes at me over my head and through my body. I know every knife stab in intimate detail and the pain and horror that comes with it.

It is 2:47 AM...and the red digital numbers light up in my eyes.

Once again, I had just dozed off for 15 minutes. I now understand that I am in my bed and have, as usual, been sleeping for only 15 minutes. The last time I looked at the clock was 2:32 AM. And yet those 15 minutes of dreams were filled with pure horror and experienced as a whole unforgettable eternity. An eternity where I remember every horrible detail that lingers like a series of photographs or a movie burned on the retina. Fifteen minutes and yet I feel an eternity and infinity of pain. At the same time, a feeling of limitless consuming and loneliness also fills me, as another night is added to the line of all the other lonely nights I've already been through.

I curl up in a fetal position as usual, rolling up like a little hedgehog. Trying to hold myself, contain myself. My body is still shaking from the horror I felt in the dream. I still feel my continued interrupted breathing, which gradually calms down. My heart is still pumping, pounding, and rushing fiercely. As usual, after one of these dreams, I try to "burn away" the memories and in retrospect reconstruct and replace the pictures from my dream in order to escape the slaughter at the very last moment - mostly by giving myself wings in the dream so I can manage to fly away from those who want to hurt me. I "simply" reconstruct the dream so I can escape from those trying to kill me. I flee from the pain and from the blood and the slaughter. Every night I flee.

My heart continues to rush even as the sweat slowly dries. The sheets feel cold and damp. It is sticky to my skin. I freeze and crawl closer to my husband who continues to sleep deeply as if nothing happened. Every night I am tortured. Murdered. And I'm slaughtered right next to him.

So much blood.
So much fear.
So much pain.

My husband doesn't notice anything. He sleeps peacefully as if nothing has happened. I get out of bed, eager to leave the ice cold, damp sheets. My feet are freezing on the floor. I am going to the toilet for what feels like the 10th time this night. I take a glass of water. Everything is very familiar. This night is just as any other night.

It's quiet and everyone except me is asleep. I move in a quiet and familiar way in the dark, over the cold floors in the apartment. My movements are really slow, as though the echo of my nightmare makes everything go in slow motion. I walk into my beloved children´s bedroom and lie next to them, one at a time for a while. Listening to their soft sniffing. Feeling their warm little bodies. Crawling close, very close. Trying to get some of the warmth and calm they radiate. I know I will not be able to fall asleep again.

The panic, the resignation and the hopelessness are like familiar uninvited guests, constantly recurring. They are uninvited, yet always by my side during all those dark and lonely hours when I am awake. They come as an "echo" after the nightmares, to keep me company whether I like it or want it or not. Due to my long experience, I know I am done sleeping this night as well. The fear and panic prevent me from falling asleep. Because, if I fall asleep, maybe I will return to the nightmare again. Feel the same nightmare over again. Experience the same horrible dreams.

I go for yet another round in the apartment. The pale moon is shining through the windows, casting long shadows in the room. My cold feet move silently, and I walk slowly on the cold floor. I am going yet again to the kitchen. I am drinking another glass of water. Going to the toilet again. Listening to the different sounds of the night. They are different from the daytime sounds.

I return to my cold part of the bed. I lay close to my husband, waiting in silence for the rest of this night to end. The feeling of helplessness and a desolate loneliness become my companions during these last hours in the dark and silent night. It is also very familiar. Everything is scary and familiar.

I shut my eyes and all the world drops dead; I lift my eyes, and all is born again.
Sylvia Plath

Pills

It is several hours later. It's still quiet and my husband and kids are sleeping. I'm lying silently curled up in my fetal position next to my husband. The dark, long and lonely hours of the night have been replaced by yet another grey and colorless day that has slowly begun. A new day. Still the same as any other grey day. I hear the sounds of my neighbors slowly waking up, living their normal lives. Like nothing has happened to me this night. Or any other night.

The rain whips against the windows. The wind causing the windows to rattle.
I'm so tired. So *damn tired.*
Tired right into my *bone marrow.*
How did I manage to get through another day?
How do I continue *to live* like this?
This paralyzing fatigue that permeates me. Day after day. Week after week. So incredibly tired.

I get out of bed and walk into the bathroom, where I find myself in front of the bathroom mirror and I can barely meet myself. I can barely look into my own eyes. I am filled with so much self-contempt. So much self-loathing. I feel so much pain. Once again, this is very familiar to me. It all reflects back to me in the mirror. I see the magnitude of the suffering. It is so raw, so intense. It isn't pretty. This sense of self-indulgence that fills every cell throughout my whole body. The visible self-contempt that invites more uninvited guests such as *meaninglessness* and *hopelessness*. So familiar. There is no escaping from the reflection in the mirror.

- How do I look?
- Who is she? The weary and tormented *Human Being* who I am looking at in the mirror?
- Who is she with the lifeless glow in her eyes? With the resigned look in her face?
- Who is this? What is this?

As always, I get scared when I see my own reflection. I open the bathroom cabinet to avoid looking at myself. Instead, I see all the medicine cans and pills that are placed next to each other.

Pills "For depression".
Pills "For sleeping disorders".
Pills "For panic and anxiety".
Pills "For pain".

But there are also other assorted cans, pills and eczema creams and lotions that have my name printed on them. I take out the can with pills "For sleeping disorders". I am holding it in my hand, feeling the smoothness of the plastic in my hand, reading the text over and over again. Without even understanding what I am reading. It just doesn't go into my brain.

I pour a lot of pills into my hand. My hand is shaking. There are many pills. So many. They are weightless in my shaking hand. It would be so easy to take them. I feel such a strong urge to take all the pills in my hand. To take them and rinse them down with water, one pill at a time, one by one. To swallow them, letting them slip down my throat. Just to be able to sleep.

I'm so devilishly tired. So really, really tired of feeling tired, being tired and exhausted all the time! I cannot stand it anymore. I don't want to feel like this. I don't want to live like this any longer. Life is meaningless and feels completely meaningless. And I have felt like this for too long now ...

I just want to take all of the small and light pills and get some sleep. To beat the tiredness. To simply fall asleep. And never wake up any more.

Releasing all the tiredness.
Releasing all the fatigue.
Releasing all the over thinking.
Releasing all the pain and the suffering.
Releasing all the worries.
Releasing all the horrible nightmares.
Releasing all the hopelessness.
Releasing all the desolation.
Releasing the *complete* and compact loneliness.

It would be so easy. Just a couple of pills away. Just to fall asleep with no more lying sleepless all alone every night. No more tiredness. What a relief it would be!

I can't live like this any longer. And I can't stand to meet another grey and heavy day.

The grey hopeless days that reflect my interior.
Would anyone even bother if I were dead, or alive?
What is the meaning of my life?
What is the meaning of this life?
What have I done to feel like this?
Why me?

I am looking down at the white pills in my hand. There are so many. They are weightless, but I still feel them all in the palm of my shaking hand. Their weight in my palm is nothing compared to the heavy weight I am carrying inside of me. Are these pills going to help me to fill my deep, bottomless inner black hole? Are they going to relieve my numbness?

- Is it now I should take all these pills?
- Is this the day I'm going to end my life?
- Is this the day when I am going to leave my beloved ones?
- Is it this day I'm going to give in to tiredness, to fall asleep, and sleep and sleep until I die?
- Would I even know the difference of sleeping or dying? I have this deep, really deep, aching longing for sleep. To fall asleep. To be asleep.

- What´s the alternative?
- What are my options?
- How will I be able to cope with more days like this?

I meet my own miserable eyes in the mirror again with a look of self-contempt and disgust. I hear how my son cries softly in his sleep. "Mom?" he cries softly for me.

After one final gaze filled with disdain I turn around and throw away all the pills into the trash bin. I leave the bathroom, close the door and move silently to attend to my son to give him what´s left of me. Once again, he has been there for me, saving me unknowingly. Once again, he has been like a lifeline for me. My beloved children. The only thing left that keeps me standing, keeps me going. My children, the only ones who keep me alive. They are my "lifelines". My beloved beautiful innocent children. I love them so much.

Deep into that darkness peering, long I stood there, wondering, fearing, doubting, dreaming dreams no mortal ever dared to dream before.

Edgar Allan Poe

Small, soft, chubby warm children's arms

An ordinary morning. One of many grey hopeless mornings where the dark and lonely hours of the night are replaced by everyday chores. Everything is the same. Same thing, same feeling. Only the dates that change show me that time is running, passing. Same, but different.

So incredibly and indescribably tired! This day has just begun, and already I feel completely leached, drained and extremely easily irritated. Very sensitive to both lights and sounds - and as usual I feel exhausted. It feels like I am constantly on the verge of breaking, crashing. Like a volcano that is constantly preparing for a massive eruption, but which does not have the ability to explode. It feels like I don´t have the power to live. However, from this space I am trying to meet my children with patience and as much love as I possibly can. I do the best I can with the limited resources I have.

I'm everywhere and nowhere, all over the place, all the time. Fragmented, both in thoughts and in movements. Fragmented in life. Like an old junkie with an uncoordinated, jerky movement pattern. I have to really concentrate, to focus for the words to come out right. My tongue feels abnormal and somehow it gets in the way when I speak.

All the time I have a feeling that time is never enough.
All the time a feeling that I am never enough.
That my love for my children is not enough.
That I am not good enough.
All the time this consuming and corrosive feeling of
inadequacy.

For as long as I can remember I have had this hollowness, this cold emptiness inside. It is a scary, creepy, dark, and bottomless black hole that is consuming me. It is eating me alive. It wears me down. It is killing me slowly, day by day. The black hole inside of me is slowly but steadily sucking the life out of me. I am so scared of this black hole that I need to fill it with something - anything. I need to find a distraction.

So, I keep myself busy by creating chores, doing activities, being occupied, constantly moving.

I clean and pick stuff up. Move it around. Re-move it. Forgetting about the stuff, forgetting things. Forgetting what I move around and where I am going. Doing the same things several times. I flutter like a trembling leaf, back and forth between the rooms, aimlessly and without structure, meaning or goals. And without any memory. I am like Doris the fish, from "Finding Nemo". In a non-funny, stressful and very dysfunctional way.

I am always starting with a chore or a task. Interrupting that chore, remembering and doing something else, starting over on another thing, another chore, another task. Starting with something new. I take out the vacuum cleaner and vacuum clean manically. Up to seven times per day. I go on my usual visits to the bathroom cabinet, and to all the pills. Looking into the mirror, meeting my tormented look, over and over again, filled with disgust.

I prepare the breakfast, help the kids with their clothes, listen to their happy and occasionally bright children's voices, their happy banter and laughter. I ask them to hurry up so we can get to pre-school. The little girl who sings loudly and cheerfully and whose voice is like a drill. Drilling, drilling, drilling into my tired, fog-filled brain. I need to get rid of the unexpected and loud sounds. I hear myself nagging, snapping with a sharp and harsh voice. They have to hurry! Rush. Rush. Quick now. We have to hurry! I am always in a hurry, always feeling the urge to rush.

"Mom …" It is my beloved son. At the time about three years old. "Mom"…
He pulls softly at my sweater and wants my attention. I'm looking down at my son. Seeing his beautiful, innocent, happy blue eyes. His beautiful eyes that really see me and penetrates me. It feels like he is looking straight into me. He looks at me in a way that I am not used to, a pure look, a pure love from loving clear blue eyes. It feels like he can see my ugliness and my tiredness. I feel ashamed over what he sees in me. I hear his soft, childish voice. "Mom…"

I respond annoyingly and the voice comes out much harsher than I intended. Much sharper than I wanted it to be. My voice is harsh, cold and sharp:

"SSSCCHHH! I have told you that I want you to be silent! I can't bear to hear anything. Do you have to talk so loudly? What is it? What do you want? We have to hurry ..."

Small soft, chubby, warm children's arms that hug me. My son hugs my legs as I am standing. This embrace makes me stop, feeling something else rather than fatigue, tiredness, hopelessness and meaninglessness - if just for a moment. Small, soft warm children's arms that hug me, who want to give me their attention, appreciation and love. Small, soft warm and innocent children's arms that touch me in the depth of my heart. A hint of something other than my usual misery. A warm sensation, a warm kind of feeling, a softness within. The moment lingers for a while and I allow myself to be included, embedded, and embraced by it.

With a soft, gentle, childish voice, my son hugs me and say: "I just want to say I love you mom ... I love you mom!". I turn away with burning tears in my eyes, grab his small, warm, loving hand and we are hurrying. Rushing off to preschool.

> *Did you really want to die? No one commits suicide because they want to die.*
> *Then why? Because they*
> *want to end the pain.*
> **Author unknown**

Everyday Life

I left the children at the preschool some time ago. When I get back home again, I find my home key left in the front door. Well, was that where it was? I hadn't even noticed that it was gone. I am so used to losing, misplacing and forgetting things that I hardly even react to it anymore.

I find myself once again walking like a drifting spirit, around and around in the apartment. Doing my rounds. Picking up toys and other stuff left by the children. I fold a little laundry. I do the beds. I pick up a dust grain from the floor. Vacuuming. I look around as if I am looking for - or searching for something, anything; without seeing anything special or in particular.

I am thinking a million thoughts without understanding or even noticing my thoughts which are fragmented into a million pieces. I don't even remember what I am thinking. And I don't even have the ability to reflect upon the quick, disturbing and stressed thoughts that pass through me. I'm just so used to them that I don't even notice them. This is *Everyday Life* to me.

I also take many turns past the bathroom cabinet and I open my many pill cans. I hold the pills in my hand for a while and feel the lightness of them. Then I pour all of them back into the cans and jars only to continue to move around uneasily and restlessly around the empty apartment.

Restless to the bones.
Worried to the bone marrow.
Nervous, constantly.

I am on the run, on the move, fleeing, escaping something I am not even aware of. Unconscious of my behavior, unconscious of my choices, unconscious of my reactions and my actions.

I didn´t even have the consciousness at the time to understand that I'm worried, restless and nervous! It's something I've come to understand - that I was always constantly restless, worried and nervous. It has taken me many decades to realize and understand that many of these negative emotions arise from anxiety. The devastating and draining feeling of anxiety that I couldn´t bear to feel, to face, to acknowledge and understand. Anxiety that I wanted so badly to escape from. It caused me to constantly rush, to hurry, to flee.

It was anxiety that made me speed up at the gym to "whip" myself even more mercilessly. At the gym I counted calories and exercised really hard, only trying to fool myself that I could escape my anxiety. All the time doing supersets, effective and purposeful, like the personal trainer I am. To keep myself on a hard, irreconcilably hard leash. Struggling and trying to free myself. To be liberated.

Anxiety that came from my inner black hole. One of the reasons for me to escape into cleaning my home meticulously over and over again. Anxiety that caused me to always be on the move mentally or physically. On the run. Doing and taking action. Being occupied with this or that. Slowly and thoroughly being consumed, eaten alive by anxiety, fear, and my black hole.

Slowly and painfully dying inside.

So stupid really, when I think about it here and now - from this space, this experience, this knowledge that I have now! Never escaping my inner reality, my inner realm – because obviously, everywhere I went it was there with me. In me. The world is never big enough to escape your inner realm, your inner reality. But at the time, I actually believed that it would vanish or dissolve by itself if only I did a little bit more. Performed a little bit more. And a little more. And a little bit more after that.

- *It was how I used to have it.*
- *It was my life, as I knew it.*

I was so used having these kinds of feelings and this sense of doing that it was my normal state of being. This urge. This need to keep on doing something all the time. So many 'musts' and 'should do´s'. Trying to keep control, stay in control. Having an illusionary sense of control. How I should look? How I should be? How should life be? If I just …

Long walks. Cleaning, vacuuming, exercising hard at the gym, looking at the mirror filled with self-hatred. Repeat. Long walks. Cleaning, vacuuming, exercising hard at the gym, looking at the mirror filled with self-hatred. Repeat…

Doesn´t everyone experience it like this?
Is there even anything else?
Could life be something other than this?

With my usual determination, I made changes to my diet and lost eight kilos while I "whipped myself hard" by exercising at the gym. I did this while I was still breastfeeding my daughter, who was even with me at the gym. For the first time ever, in my 34 year-old life, I was actually satisfied with the way I looked. Only six months after my daughter's birth I had a "six-pack" on my flat stomach. My arms, shoulders and legs were strong and lean, with well-defined muscles.

On the outside, it seemed like I had it all. A beautiful family, healthy kids, a loving husband, a beautiful strong body and a good job. I was employed as a Physiotherapist with my own Company where I worked as an Aerobic and Yoga Instructor and Personal Trainer. Basically, a wonderful life travelling around the globe. People often told me how 'lucky' I was.

But my inner, invisible world, was full of chaos and disorder. My whole everyday life circulated around worrying about my lack of sleep and my attempts to try and control my weight. To control my life in every way I possibly could. But the bottomless and everlasting feeling that I was being hunted, pursued me both day and night. Twenty-four-seven. I felt haunted day and night, regardless of any activity, task, job, situation, or even when surrounded by loved ones. Haunted for all those grey meaningless days and all those bottomless and lonely dark nights.

And I was always chasing; begging for praise and admiration from everyone in my environment:

- *Am I being good enough?*
- *Am I alright?*
- *Do I look ok?*
- *Do you like me?*

I did get a lot of praise from the people around me. They said that I looked good, was being strong and looked lean in my body so short a time after my pregnancy. Many hours were spent at the gym when the children were at preschool and when my husband was working. Many hours were spent cleaning, doing, moving myself - and things - around and around.

My reflection now, ten years later, is that this was just some of my ways. Some of my many strategies to handle *Anxiety* and *Fear.* And I wasn't even aware of this at the time. Aware that I had so much anxiety and so many fears inside of me. My behavior was like that of a "junkie".

I was completely fragmented, with a jerky movement pattern. My coordination was affected, and my concentration was barely non-existent.

I was also extremely sensitive to both sound and light. The smallest unexpected sounds made me jerk. Being startled by phone signals that cut into my ears and made me jump every time the phone rang. When the children played and laughed loudly, I went after them, telling them that they should be silent. Telling them not to make too much noise.

Not to talk or laugh so loudly. As soon as someone dropped something on the floor, I got irritated and frustrated by the noise. I often walked around wearing earplugs and earmuffs at home. Feeling like a volcano that was about to burst; ready to explode! I never understood why I felt like this or reacted like this.

Of course, I know I love my kids!
I love and adore them. They are my biggest gifts, my biggest achievement.
However, I cannot F E E L the Love.
How does love feel?
Where is love supposed to be felt in the body?
I know love is there, but I cannot feel the love for my children, or my husband. For anyone.

All these grey days that seem to float together. The dark nights that float together. Days and nights, nights and days. Everything is sort of floating together, glued together and it becomes a blur. Life is blurred. My life is - and feels like - a long, lonely and meaningless thick fog that is draped around me; around everything. It´s preventing me from seeing or understanding anything except or beyond the fog.

Days and nights are passing by. My life is passing me by, and everything seems to be repeated. It just plays over and over again. Life is, and feels like, my long nightmares. And it´s like it´s never going to end. Endless days, endless nights, endless nightmares, endless fog. Endless suffering.

I am afraid and anxious of being alone in the day.
I am afraid and anxious to go to bed at night.
I am afraid of going to bed and having the same terrible nightmares every night where I am being chased, tortured, slaughtered, slayed and murdered.

These horrendous pictures are chasing me and hunting me day and night. I am afraid of these dreams that I have every night and the way I wake up all sweaty and disoriented, with the metallic blood taste in my mouth and my rushing, pumping heart. These nightmares where I always wake up with a silent scream at 2:47 AM, with the red digital numbers in my eyes. Night after night. The same desolate loneliness and sense of hopelessness in these grey and hopeless days that are my life.

So, I tried to "keep my life together". It was like my whole existence depended on that. To keep myself together. I tried to contain and control myself. To hide my inner chaotic self from the outside world. Shutting down. Trying to distance and suppress 'myself' from myself - and also others. Just so it all would look good on the outside. Setting up a mask where "everything is good".

I have played many roles in my life. Apparently, I was very good at playing roles and acting. Nobody ever seemed to notice my inner struggle. Nobody seemed to suspect what was actually going on within. Nobody even asked me: "How are you really?" So, I kept on struggling. It was like a never-ending inner fight that went on and on, very present inside of me, but maybe not so visible or noticeable to others. I didn´t know about anything else. Couldn't do it any other way but fighting and struggling.

Fighting - that's good. That, I can do. I know how to do it and also that I "should" continue to do so. From my Finnish inheritance, I have 'Sisu', which means never ever giving up. So, I always keep fighting just as the Finnish people fought against the Russians in the Finnish winter war.

I often hear from people in my surroundings that I have everything - and that people look up to me. That I am so fortunate and so lucky that they envy me. What do they really know? This has left me feeling anxious and with a huge internal stress. I NEVER felt that I was sufficient or was good enough or that I did enough. Instead, I was filled with shame and guilt over having to do more; to prove myself worthy, so as to not disappoint anybody. And my mask, my cover, my protection was being even more shielded. And I felt even more distant, more separated, and very alone.

A certain deceptive "calmness" came over me when I did all these things and distracted myself by being busy. Acting busy. Unfortunately, this calmness didn't last long and this urged me to keep doing, to keep moving, keeping me being busy. The deceptive calmness really was a short escape from anxiety. Anxiety always somehow seemed to come back after the supersets at the gym - and after vacuuming the apartment or after cleaning the bathroom or walking.

But this relief becomes shorter and less felt, so I had to

constantly fill the emptiness within me. The emptiness that was growing and growing. The emptiness scared me. The emptiness and meaninglessness that grew more and more and which I tried to protect myself from and shield myself from. The less I sleep at night, the more I get done in the day. I have the illusion that it is the only way to keep the emptiness and fear away. Completely exhausted, I plunge into bed every night and believe all the time that:

"Everything is getting better soon." I MUST just do a little more.
A little more.
I just have to be a little better.
Or to lose some more weight.
I need to keep moving in order not to be engulfed.
Engulfed by something so terrifying and I can´t even understand what it is.
I just need to keep going a little more and not give up!
How do you even give up?

Every day I have this wish, this longing, just to fall asleep. Never to wake up again.

In spite of all this, I go to my work anyway. Not because I want to, or because I like it. It´s more like a "heavy duty". A must. It´s because I must fit in socially. I have to adapt, and I must go to work. Period. My job as a preschool teacher in a large preschool in a socially undeveloped area in Stockholm. The job that I dislike so incredibly much. I actually hate it and hate everything about it, except for the children.

Just by getting close to my job I get breathing difficulties. My head becomes so heavy and my body feels like it´s weighing a ton. I have such a huge resistance to go there. When I open the gate to the preschool in the morning, the whole world "shrinks", and when I enter the building it is like the roof and the walls are falling down on me with its entire weight. When I come home Friday afternoons' I get about two hours respite from the anxiety I feel - the anxiety of having to go back to work on Monday. So, my "Sunday anxiety" starts every Friday evening.

At the place I work there are many bitter colleagues and bitter managers. There are a lot of children in each group and the sound levels at the preschool is loud and intense. It is actually too loud and too intense for me as I have great sensitivity for loud sounds and noise. Many staff at my working place are burned out and many are, or have been, on sick leave. There are many women who gossip about each other and there is also a lot of "backstabbing". And the working conditions cause a lot of dissatisfaction and insecurity among those who work there. The communication between us and the managers is insufficient to say the least - and the managers have 'favorites' among the staff.

In short, in the job I do I am constantly subjected to a silent bullying that is really hard to describe. And I am exposed to being bullied both by the managers and by my colleagues. My colleagues change the conversation topic or become silent when I enter the room. They even leave the staff room when I enter. It feels very awkward, and it contributes to me feeling even more separated from myself and from others.

My managers don´t approve of, and try to limit, my right to take out the 'parental days' that I am entitled to. The feelings of guilt and being accused of something when I am at home being sick, or home with sick kids, is always present. I have a constant feeling that I do not fit in, no matter how hard I try. The kids at the preschool like me though. They come to me when they are sad, upset or when they are longing for their mother or father. They want to sit on my lap. I am being told that I should not put a sad child on my lap to comfort them for some inexplicable reason.

At the preschool I am employed to partly handle the healthcare for the staff, but my plans and ideas are never well received. There is never any money, no resources, no "need", nor time to listen to my ideas or to make improvements for the staff. So, this negative spiral just goes on. This too, is eating me alive from the inside.

At our regular job meetings, we really should be discussing why we are "down on our knees". We are not feeling well. The workload and the stress level are too high, and our well-being is getting worse. We need to address the bullying and the favoritism of some people above others. Instead of addressing the real important topics, the whole unit sits for hours and hours, discussing meaningless things such as where the bread baskets should be put. And the pros and cons of why they should be where they are. And on top of everything, everyone must actively participate in this meaningless discussion. Then we all need to agree. It´s such an incredible waste of time and energy. It is making my entire body restless and I am twisting like a worm on a hook where I sit.

I can´t help but to reflect how strangely and inefficiently we are using the money payed by us tax payers. We avoid discussing the important, and the delicate issues. The topics that really would make a difference for us, for the children, and for the whole unit. We avoid the topics like how to reduce our workload and how to increase our well-being. We don´t talk about how to deal with the bullying and the back-stabbing. We avoid talking about how we really feel and what we really need. If I ever mention something that feels important, or something of the bullshit and bullying that happen in the yard, people lower their eyes, shrug and get very silent. And I sit there in the awkward silence feeling very exposed and under the scrutiny of everybody. I also feel very alone even though I know that many of my colleagues share my point of view - but they don´t dare to express it in front of the managers.

Everyday some, and sometimes many, of my colleagues are home on sick leave. We are very unhealthy in our team with all sorts of stress related symptoms, such as headache, migraine, pain in the body and burnouts. We very rarely get substitute staff to cover for the ones that are sick. There is a constant high workload - especially with large children's groups - and a lot of noise. I have never been to a workplace where so many of the staff are on sick leave for various reasons. We are more often under-staffed than being fully staffed. It is wearing us down in every way and it is extremely boring. It's so boring so the clocks seem to be frozen. I look at the clock several times every hour and think that time is hardly passing:

"Now it's only 5 hours and 47 minutes before I can go home."

So, it is the same every day. *Everyday.* Everybody is complaining when out in the yard, but nobody is addressing this, nobody is managing it, nobody cares. Especially not the managers.

Other unpleasant things that happen at work are that my colleagues and managers change my schedule without informing me. It gets trickier to get my daily life puzzle together with my children, husband and caring for my home. The job schedule constantly changes, suddenly and without a warning. I also become "stationed" where no one else wants to be. Often in the outdoor yard and also often alone with lots of screaming children. The others are inside and "documenting". I contact the teachers' union on a number of occasions when I feel unfairly treated and I dare not meet the managers alone. Or when I have not received the pay rise I know I am entitled to.

I'm dragging myself to work.
Dragging myself home.
Day after day. Same, same.
Dragging myself through life.
Feeling more dead than alive.
My sanctuary is with my family.
My children.
My beloved ones who keep me up.
Those who keep me alive.
I am here physically, but still not here.
Don't know where I am.
Or who I am.
What is the meaning of life?

I'm thinking that all of this will turn around, change, soon enough. I'm just going to keep track so that I don't gain weight. I probably need to take another turn with the vacuum cleaner. I need to and I MUST just endure this a little bit more, or maybe even try a little bit harder. Every day starting anew, every night closing this day and going into the nightmares. Creating my *Everyday Life,* over and over again.

All that we are is the result of what we have thought. The mind is everything. What we think we become.

Buddha

Ullis 34 years old, feeling like 134 …

I am ill?

I have been with my therapist for a long time. And I have been approved to see a therapist from the municipal psychiatric care center in Sweden. We pay quite high taxes, but our schools and health care are also included together with the other benefits of being a Swedish taxpayer.

One day my therapist tells me I'm ill. Really ill. That I should be on sick leave. That I need to rest. Take it easy. Slow down. Think about myself and my health. She looks at me with a worried and deeply concerned look. It cuts me like a knife when I meet her friendly but worried eyes. I shy away from her eyes. I can't cope with that look.

"I am ill?"

I do not feel sick. I have no cold, no fever. I don't have pain anywhere. I'm rarely ill. And rest? Slowing down. I don't know what that is or how to even do it. Resting for me is going to the gym or slowing down when taking a long walk. Although I sometimes have a cold, a fever or a pain, I still go to work out of pure duty. I just take some painkillers, and then I go to work. After all, it will soon pass. Having a cold and going to work is not something that you die from. Doesn´t everybody who is sick just take a pill of some sort and still go on? Going to work I mean.

"Well, ill?"

Not me.
As I said, I am never sick. I don´t feel ill. But then, I think it might be good to be home for a while. At least I don't have to go to my work that I don't like anyway. I can be home from work one week and be ill. Fine with me.

The one week I was supposed to be at home "being ill" turned weirdly and totally unexpectedly into actually staying at home for several weeks. I was so tired that, for the first time in my life, I was unable to go to the gym or to work. Actually, I wasn´t even able to get out of bed for many days over the following weeks. Very often the fatigue was so massive and so compact that I had to make an effort to keep my tongue straight in my mouth so that I would not stutter when I talked. These weeks at home on sick leave eventually grew in number and in some funny, unexpected way, became months.

Months that came and passed as if in a haze, like in a fog. The same; same but different. These months that eventually turned into a year. I had so many different stress related symptoms that my doctor said I was both depressed and burned-out. That one year turned into a very long year - and many years followed of feeling separated, excluded, alone and like an outsider.

Outside work.
Outside security.
Outside society.
Out of life.
Life outside.
Outside life.
The feeling of isolation.
Not to be seen.
Not to exist.
Loneliness.

The devastating feeling of separation. Being separated. The imminent sense of separation, even when I spend time with family and friends which I came to recognize so well during those years. The shame. And the blame of being so freaking weak so I wasn´t READY to work. The shame and the guilt that I couldn´t even sleep like a normal person.

This 'one week' that my therapist suggested that I stayed home from work became one of many years. It gave me a heavy feeling that I was "a burden on society", with a lot of guilt and shame and yet, still fighting, struggling, and resisting. I continued to "fight" against all my struggles. I "fought" against the fatigue that paralyzed me. So, I struggled and still made the effort: going to the gym: exercising, cooking, leaving the kids at preschool, picking them up again and cleaning a little more. Being in control. Keeping the weight steady. Doing a little more.

I had a hard time accepting and realizing, that my body was run down. I had no more power, no more resources within me. And then, on top of everything, all these endless phone calls with contacts at *Försäkringskassan* (the government institute in Sweden that administers payments to people on sick leave funded by all of us who pay tax in Sweden). They had no compassion and no understanding whatsoever. But they needed to follow the rules and regulations of course.

All these conversations when I was transferred here and there. Where I got new contact persons, administrators and doctors. I had to repeat everything, telling them the same story, over and over again. All those hours of waiting in phone queues just to be disconnected, or to hear that the person couldn't take my call today. It was completely draining me of the little energy I had left. All of these different time-consuming and energy-intensive contacts with various levels of understanding and ignorant doctors.

"No, I'm still not sleeping.
No, there is no change.
No, I haven't got over it yet unfortunately."

The very recognizable feeling of guilt and shame. The sense of being a burden for everyone. Never being enough. Not at work.

Not for my family. Not for anything. Some of the diagnoses I was given, by the doctors were:

IBS (Irritable bowel syndrome)
Constipation
Seasonal depression
Fatigue Depression
Burn-out
Anxiety
Panic attacks
Eczema
Sleeping disorders
Concentration Interference
Memory Disorders
Extremely sound and light sensitiveness

The expression, "you have to be healthy to be sick" turned out to be so true in all those endless conversations with doctors, administrators, contact persons and managers. It took me a lot of time and energy just to get in touch with these people and to get the right documents. To express to them how I felt but knowing that they didn´t really hear me, didn´t see me, nor understand me. I didn´t even feel that they cared about me.

And all the time the feeling that my life and my financial security were in someone else's hands all the time, - the hands of Försäkringskassan. Was I ill enough or sick enough to get my sick leave approved? And could it be possibly extended as the months and the years passed by? New phone calls, new documents, new contact persons; but same old story. And then the threat of constantly being denied the little money I was entitled to. My experience of the doubt in their voices:

"Are you still depressed/burned-out?"
"What are your illnesses again?"
"How long have you been at home now?"

To me those questions hit me like a hard punch in my face and they felt more like:

"Why don't you want to work?"
"What is wrong with you?"
"Why don´t you get a grip of yourself?"
"Is she lying?"
"Is she speaking the truth?"
"Is she just being lazy?"
"Does she know she is a burden on society?"

A doctor once said to me: "You, who are so good looking and sweet, you cannot possibly have any troubles at all!" And also: "It will probably pass by itself. I will just prescribe you a little more medication."

During my many meetings with various doctors, I suggested several alternatives to my own treatment. I proposed '*Light Therapy*'. '*Sleep School*'. '*Talk therapy*'. Even something called the '*Stress Rehabilitation program*'. All the time the medication and pills were being generously offered and generously subscribed to me, even though I told them I wasn´t interested in just medications. I wasn´t interested in just removing or relieving the symptoms. I wanted to get into - and get rid of - the root cause of my many symptoms, my depression, and my burn-out. Why was I feeling like this in the first place? Still, medications were given to me, without me even asking for them.

Sleeping pills.
Pills for Insomnia.
Pills for Serotonin-enhancement.
Pills for anxiety.
Pills for this and that.
Supplements.
Vitamins.
Cortisone creams and lotions for my burning eczema.

These were the cans and jars of medicines and pills that were lining up in my bathroom cabinet and which filled and occupied all of my thoughts. It filled me and occupied me all my waking hours - both day and night. My whole life revolved around these pills. Like a moth that revolves around the light.

The real meaning of enlightenment is to gaze with undimmed eyes on all darkness.
Nikos Kazantzakis

My little baby girl

One morning, when I had already taken my son to his preschool, and I am about to make myself and my little baby girl prepared for a meeting I had with a doctor in the city, I feel very stressed. This morning I am in an unusual "hurry". Someone is calling me on the phone, and it is ringing loudly through the whole apartment. The loud and sharp noise from the phone is cutting through my ears. The echo of the sharp ringing phone stays as an uncomfortable vibration in me, long after the conversation itself is over. It is like loud screaming in my ears.

This busy morning, I forget the eggs on the stove, so they explode in the pan. It smells burnt and I am afraid that the fire alarm will go off. I open the window to get rid of the stench from the eggs and I clean the stove from the mess of the exploding eggs. The stench is everywhere, and it smells incredible disgusting, like shit, really.

I dress myself, brush my teeth, and I dress my little baby girl who at the time is five to six months old. When she is ready, I leave her in her car child seat in the hallway, where she sits ready to go and happily kicking with her little legs. I stress around in the apartment while I am packing and searching for my travel card that I do not seem to find. Looking everywhere for that travel card. I can't find it. I am in a great hurry. Hurry! Hurry!

Finally, I am ready to leave the apartment. I even remembered to lock the door. I put the keys in a pocket. Because I am quite late, I need to run to the station which is five minutes away. I buy a new travel card as I didn´t find the other one. I really hope that I will make it in time to the doctor. The subway comes and I sit down on a seat. I look distractedly at the stations passing by, the thoughts are everywhere and nowhere, all over the place. As usual.

After three or four stations on the subway, I suddenly get a tingling and a disturbing sensation that there is something that I have forgotten. Something I should have remembered to remember. A vague, diffuse sense of discomfort. Something is wrong. What can it be? Is there anything I have missed? I restlessly start to move a little, where I sit trying to get rid of the feeling of discomfort.

It's something I've forgotten! Something I should remember. Something very important!
What is it that I have forgotten? Did I really turn off the stove? Did I close the window? Did I lock the door?

I look around with searching eyes, to get some kind of clue and to remember what it is I have forgotten. What can it be? Then I see it. The magnitude of my insight hits me like a knife stabbed into my heart. My baby girl is missing. She is not there next to me. Where's my little girl? Where is she? She is not next to me in her trolley. There is no trolley next to me at all.

Oh my God…where's my baby girl? Where is she? I'm having a panic attack. Cannot breathe properly. My field of view is instantly narrowing, it is like I'm looking through two thin straws. Thinking and praying intensely and repeatedly:

Please. Please. Please. Dear God. Help me to find my daughter. Help me to find my baby girl. Please help me so that nothing has happened to her. Please help me so that she is safe.
P l e a s e God. Dear God, help me!

I throw myself off at the station where the train has stopped. I manage to get out just before the doors are closing. With "unseeing eyes" I am looking around at the platform, without actually registering anything of what I see. I chew on my nails. I can feel the bottomless fear and the panic inside of me that feels like a hard, razor sharp and cold "ice floe". It feels like my heart is being held very tight, and painfully in an irreconcilable ice-cold vice.

I jump anxiously back and forth on the platform with my heart frozen stuck in the icy cold vice. My whole inner reality is ice cold, the coldest of the frozen frost. My movements feel as if in slow motion and they are very stiff, even rigid. It feels like I am "swirling away", losing the perception, both of time and space. I am here at the platform and yet I am being swept away in a massive, invisible, grey tornado, with the sensation of being in free fall. It feels like I am "zooming out". Something strange also seems to be happening with time. The time is moving so slowly, and yet it feels like it is rushing forward. Where is the subway? Why does it take so long?

When the tube finally arrives, after what feels like an eternity, I throw myself back onto the tube. I remain standing and jumping nervously as I pass all the recently passed stations and I try to think. Trying to gather my thoughts. I am probably thinking about a million thoughts but not getting hold of any of them. It all comes down to: Where is she? Where's my baby girl? My darling, where are you? I am sorry. I am sorry. I am so, so sorry!

I try really hard to remember where and when I saw her the last time, but I do not remember.

I don't remember the last time I saw her, or where it was. The memories I try to remember escape me, elude me. It´s like a fog. It is like trying to catch something, to hold on to something that slides right through my fingers. Slides through my memory. Oh my God!

- *Did I forget her on the platform?*
- *What if someone took her?*
- *What if the trolley rolled down the track?*
- *What if …?*

I return to my home station after what feels like an eternity. An eternity in complete agony. My heart is pounding as it still feels as if it is stuck in the tight grip of an icy vice. This is not only felt in the chest area but now also is in my entire body. I feel so contracted, so scared. My whole body is now locked in that razor sharp, ice-cold and hard vice.

My narrow vision scans the platform. No trolley there on the platform. No baby. I run down to stairs to the staff behind the latch, and I ask breathlessly if someone has found a trolley, or a baby left on the platform. "Has anyone found and left a baby?"

I hear that my words are expressed with a scared, loud and anxious voice. "No," the answer comes fast, "No baby. Sorry." I don't know what to do next, who to turn to. My heart bursts in complete horror in my chest and the hair on my arms are raised. Tears that make my already limited vision even more of a blur, are burning behind the eyelids.

I run home without breathing, feeling cold sweat all over me. I am finally standing in front of my front door, holding my breath. I fumble to open it. Don't seem to remember the code to the entrance. What did I do with the keys? The keys...where are the keys? I am searching frantically for the keys and with relief I find them, in the last pocket I search. I fumble with the keys in the lock to the front door, with my hands trembling both by cold but also by the indescribable horror that I feel. No trolley. No baby inside of the front door. It´s very quiet. Dead silence.

I can only hear myself gasping for breath, my panting and quick breathing. The sweat runs along my entire back, while I have inner chills and still feel cold. I feel so numb within. Like I am shut off, shut down. Like I am the living dead. I cannot feel the keys I hold in my hand. My shaky hands fumble again with the lock to the front door of the apartment.

Finally.
Oh my God! There she is!!!
My little baby girl is sitting there in the hallway, exactly where I left her. She is still dressed, ready to go. She is still waiting for her mother. Waiting for me. She's silent and still. She sits there silently looking at me with her beautiful big innocent eyes as

I open the door and step into the hallway. An immense sense of gratitude fills me!!! There she is, my little girl sitting there, silently waiting for me in the trolley. My little girl. I am really, truly grateful that she is there. She is ok, she is alive!

- *Thank you, God!*
- *Thank You!*
- *Thank You!*
- *Thank You!*

I collapse in a pile beside her. I take her little warm body into my arms and I am sitting with my jacket and shoes still on and just rock her back and forth in my arms. We are sitting in silence. Our bodies are close, really, really close. I can feel her warm sweet smelling, soft breath on my forehead. My tears pour down on my cheeks with a burning sensation. I let them run freely, barely noticing them. We stay really close to each other, with our bodies intertwined and in silence for the rest of the afternoon. Me and my little baby girl. We sit for hours until it is time to go and pick up her big brother from preschool. We sit in complete silence, with the clothes still on. We sit very close, tightly together and with my burning tears flowing endlessly, like a warm gentle stream, over my face.

The panic and horror in my heart stayed there for a very, very long time after this episode as well as the ice cold feeling of being stuck in that tight, hard vice. It has etched itself into my memory, etched into my heart and my soul. The feeling of not being able to trust myself or my memory is still very hard, embarrassing and difficult to explain. Even more difficult to understand! How could I lose or forget about my own child?

This night, for the first time in a very, very long time, I did not wake up from my nightmares.

Because I never fell asleep. The guilt, shame and self-contempt I felt on that evening is one of the most painful things I have ever experienced. And the raw pain kept me awake all night.

How could I forget my own child, my baby girl? How hard can a human being fall? I didn´t know that it was even possible for me to fall this hard.

- *What is wrong with me?*
- *What the hell is wrong with me?*

I went through this thought, I felt the pain and the suffering, I tortured myself in my mind over and over again as it just kept repeating, repeating and repeating itself. I experienced the panic when she was not in the trolley beside me a million times that night. It was a very, very long, lonely and painful night. It was by far my longest and most lonely night ever. Of all those long and lonely nights that I had experienced in my life, this was the worst.

I never told anyone there and then about this event. I was simply so ashamed, so full of guilt and I thought, and felt, that I was a worthless mother. But the memory, and the feelings this situation caused, were, as I mentioned, long-lasting. The echo of the pain I felt this night lingered as an unwelcome deep wound that has been hidden deep within. It pains me just to think about it. To share it with you, writing about this here and now.

Even though it has been many years ago now, I can still remember the echo of this long, lonely, horrible shameful night, full of self-contempt. The feeling of complete failure while being filled with self-hatred at the same time.

Some days, 24 hours is too much to stay in, so I take the day hour by hour, moment by moment. I break the task, the challenge, the fear into small bite-size pieces. I can handle a piece of fear, depression, regret, pain, sadness, loneliness, illness. I actually put my hands up to my face, one next to each eye, like blinders on a horse.

Regina Brett

The desire to rest

The days and nights go by intertwined with, and entangled, into each other. As one grey day ends, the lonely, dark night begins. They are connected into each other, into a haze, a maze, a mess. They move on slowly and thickly like a cloudy river. My everyday life, and my whole life is just moving on. Passing me by. The cloudy river of my life. Without any endings. Without even any beginnings.

The agony and the anxiety every day, as well as the misery and the suffering every night of not being able to sleep. All those dark nights that come with nightmares and loneliness. The black hole inside of me sucking me in, consuming me, killing me slowly, but surely. The constant restlessness, and the need to be doing something all the time, every day. The feeling that I have to do something, keep moving, keep myself slim, be busy, keep going. Otherwise… otherwise what? What else is there?

The long, lonely sleepless nights. The horrible nightmares between 02:32-02:47 AM that I am used to waking up from, escaping them with silent screams. My heart rushing and the stale taste of blood in my mouth. Lying awake, all alone and in silence before 02:32. Then waking up at 02:47, after the nightmare, staying awake with desolation and horror as my only single companion that lasts until dawn. The thoughts that all of this must come to an end. That today, this day that is about to begin, is going to be my last day. Last day to live. Last night to being awake.

Life that gradually becomes smaller and smaller. A life shrinking, a shrinking life. My life that is getting narrower and narrower. Like a prison. Life in a prison. My life as being locked up, hidden in a dungeon. Life slowly but inexorably shrinking to nothing. And yet, my thoughts are being occupied by the insomnia. What to do, how to cope? It permeates everything and becomes nothing. The thoughts that are nothing - but yet take everything that is worth something in my life. To a nothingness, a "nothing-mess". My life being a mess, shrinks to less than nothing, and the hopelessness grows.

My memories of these days, these weeks, these months, and years are often blurred. Fuzzy. Like a heavy, dense grey mist that takes over and eats up everything that is alive within me and around me. I didn't really know how to get through all these days and nights. I couldn't see a solution. However, I do remember the constant feelings of emptiness, desolation, futility and the endless overwhelming fatigue. The fatigue that seems to come from within the bone marrow, which I cannot escape from, cannot rest from. Just a heavy paralyzing fatigue. The feeling of being constantly chased and tormented. A man hunt, and I am the wanted one. I remember the suffering and tormented gaze that met me in the bathroom mirror every morning. Eyes that were more dead than alive. The lifeless look I saw several times a day. Then the ubiquitous presence and longing to end everything. The desire to rest. The desire, the longing to just fall asleep. The desire to be asleep. The desire to die. The desire to avoid living. Not to live like this anymore.

And yet, somewhere parallel and unconscious, there is a

small, barely discernible spark. Strange enough, but yet still a spark of desire to live! A small little invisible unconscious desire. A longing to live full of life! A living life. A desire of being alive. Not dead, but an alive life. A desire of a whole life, a life without that defeating inner black hole. A whole life. A life of freedom, happiness and love!

Pain changes people. It makes them trust less, think more and shut people out.

Author unknown

Tonight, I can sleep. Finally...

It is a late winter night in 2007 after another day on sick leave. I sit on the couch and talk to my husband. The sound of the TV is low in the background. I am still "just" at home not doing anything - meaning not working- during the day. I have the usual visits to the gym and the long walks for burning calories. I also washed four machines, vacuumed, cleaned, picked up the kids from preschool, shopped and prepared the food.

The dinner is fixed, we have eaten, and the dishes are now done. The children are put into bed and sleep peacefully. I do not tell my husband how I really think or what I really feel. I am not telling him that I don't want to live or discuss how I can live like this any longer. My husband knows nothing about my sense of resignation and hopelessness, or how tired I really am. He knows of course that I am tired, but not how deep it goes - that it´s all-consuming, devastating, eating me alive. He only knows that I am infinitely tired. Dead tired. Every day dead tired. He does not know that life feels meaningless. He does not know about my inner battle in front of the bathroom cabinet and with the medications that I go through every day. He doesn't know about my thoughts or feelings or my desire to just take the pills and fall into asleep. My desire to fall into an eternal asleep.

Instead, when we talk, I just mention that as usual, I am really tired and that it might be good for me to go away; get an environmental change. He agrees that it would be good for me, and we surf the internet together to check out various retreat centers. Then I realize that I can ask my parents if I can go out to Ingarö in the beautiful Swedish archipelago to get some rest and some change. To be out there in the silence all by myself for a while without anything that disturbs me or prevents me from getting some rest.

Ingarö, which over time will turn out to be the most important place for me to be is like a safe haven. A safe container like a warm, soft, silent uterus where I can lay and get some rest. Ingarö - a sacred place where I can retreat and start to heal myself. This is the sacred place where I started my long and tough journey back to myself. Retrieving myself bit by bit, piece by piece. My beloved Ingarö, with its large areas of wild forests and the ocean. Where the sea and sky meet in an endless kiss and which is embraced by the serenity of pure nature.

Vastness.
Spaciousness.
Serenity.
Stillness.

It became, and has remained, my favorite place on earth. An innocent place with beautiful silence, peace and quiet.

We decided that I was to go out alone to Ingarö. So, I packed my stuff and left next morning after saying goodbye to the kids. I had never been away from them before and I started to miss them as soon as I was on the bus going out there. I was struck by the calmness and the long-awaited silence when I got off the bus. I could hear the muffled sounds of my footsteps and the soft creaking sound when I walked in the snow towards the house. That was the only thing that

I heard. I could hear and feel the sound of silence. It is a very special sound. It didn´t scare me: actually, it was very welcoming and soft in its intensity. Familiar in an unknown way. The evening was dark but bright. I could see all the stars shining from above and it was beautiful. The air was cold but felt crisp. I felt a slight concern about being there by myself, but also some kind of relief.

I walk up to the house, open the door and enter. I hang up my clothes and then I go straight ahead to turn off the TV. I also shut off the refrigerator as the soft humming from the fridge is already too much noise for my sensitive ears. It's very cold and humid inside so I wrap myself in a thick woolen blanket. I don´t light any of the lamps. I am exhausted so I go to bed, laying down in the dark. Now. Finally. Now it is very quiet and very dark, just as I want it. Just as I need. So hopefully I can fall asleep. My thoughts fly loosely and freely. I think a lot about my children and feel that I already miss their warm and soft hugs. Their childish laughter. I think about how many calories I need to burn and how many long walks I will take here. I fix the bed and when it´s done I and lay down to sleep for the night without eating dinner. I really think and I truly hope that tonight it will be better. Tonight, is going to be the night when I will fall asleep easily. Finally!

> *God has a purpose for your pain, a reason for your struggle and a reward for your faithfulness. Don´t give up.*
>
> **Dave Willis**

I am freezing inside.

I am once again being thrown with a silent scream out of my dream in horror where I was murdered this night. Slaughtered in the bathtub, as in an old "Psycho" movie.

The horrible bloody images of my own murder still burn on the retina. The sharp metallic taste of blood in the mouth and the blood rushing through my body. My heart pumps and pumps like crazy as if it's going to explode. There is a feeling of not being able to breathe properly as the breathing comes and goes in fast but shallow panting and gasps. Panic and horror that keeps my body in a tight and hard grip. The contraction in itself is very painful. The sweat varnishes my body even though it is chilly in the room. The compact darkness surrounds me and dwells inside of me. The darkness that is everywhere and fills everything.

My tremendous disappointment, and frustration, floods over me as a great flood that overflows during the rainy season; when I realize that even this night is like the other 100's of past nights that I have spent awake. I am doubting my sanity. What is wrong with me? Why can't I just fall asleep and sleep like everyone else? Why do I have to endure this suffering?

The only difference from my usual nights is that I am now "physically alone". There is no husband to crawl closer too. No warmness from my husband's body, no closeness. No children to lie close to, embracing them, listening to their soft breathing. No sense of security. Nothing except me, the darkness and the raw, damp cold. I am freezing even more when the sweat slowly dries, and my damp hair is feeling cold against my skin. The blood taste in my mouth gradually decreases, as does the heart rate that slowly slows down.

The remnants of the dream and finding myself physically alone makes me scared to death in a way I have never experienced before. I am now completely alone in the dark, waiting for the remaining hours of the cold winter's night to end. I am listening to how the hard wind outside makes the windows tremble. I wrap myself in yet another thick woolen blanket and lie tight and shriveled up in a fetal position and hold on, trying to hold myself together. Holding on to sanity. Holding on for life. Holding on, as a matter of life and death, desperately trying to keep myself together.

This windy winter night that has just started suddenly feels so long. So unbearably long and lonely. Endless. And so very dark. Bottomless and pitch black. Like my inner hole. Even if it is windy outside the compact silence is surrounding me and fills me inside. And I am freezing inside. I am alone and terrified …

> *My silence is yet another expression
> for the pain I am feeling.*
> **Author unknown**

The Snowfall

I lie silently awake just waiting for the night to end, and for the day to finally break. Hour by hour slowly passes by. I don´t move. I don´t even to go to the toilet which I actually need. I am all alone in the bed at Ingarö. It's cold, raw and damp in the room. I am still lying curled up in a fetal position with lots of thick quilts and blankets over me trying to get warm. It's cold anyway. I'm freezing. It's like this icy coldness comes from inside. An ice-cold penetrating coldness inside that fills my whole body.

Slowly, slowly, the carbon black night is replaced by a bright dawn. I get out of the cold damp bed, put on two bathrobes, a hat, a pair of gloves and thick socks and go out to the quiet and dark living room where I light a fire. I sit myself down very close to the fire to absorb the heat and to let it "defrost" my body. I stay like this for a while and I look with unseeing eyes at the flames in the fire. The heat from the fireplace eventually warms my body and softens the severe coldness I feel inside. I have no idea how long I sit there. I sit for a while even after the fire has gone out, without even noticing it.

When I do experience that the fire has gone out and that the heat has disappeared. I notice that it looks like it´s going to be a beautiful winter day out there. The snow is sparkling white and it glitters like diamonds when the sun is reflected on it. Winter blue sky and a beautiful winter sun. Feathery snowflakes, that catch the light as they fall down softly, like those in a glass ball that you turn upside down to create a winter landscape.

I'm getting ready to go out. I prepare and eat my breakfast without actually being aware of how it tastes. I don´t even remember what I ate. My sense of smell has been gone for a long time and my taste buds are also blunted and numb. I don't taste the flavors so clearly anymore. It's nothing I consciously think of or am aware of. That's just the way it is. And it has been like this for some time now.

I randomly walk around, looping between the rooms. I have the feeling of something unidentifiable inside, something stirring, moving up from the inner black hole. Something unrecognizable. Intangible. It is difficult to put my finger on what it is. It scares me though and makes me anxious and nervous; restless. I don´t know what it is, but it makes me increase my pace. I move quicker through the rooms. I pick up something that has fallen on the floor. As though by doing something and being active will help me in trying to understand what it is that I feel inside. The urge of doing something to flee from something else. There is a familiar feeling of impatience and restlessness. Like there's something I'm waiting for. I don´t even know this or understand what it is that I am waiting for. I have to do something. I have to go out. It feels better if I take a long and quick walk and burn a lot of calories. It usually does. At least for a short while. I have to get away from this 'something' inside of me that feels like it's chasing me: haunting me. Makes me want to crawl out of my own skin just trying to escape it.

This something is scary, unrecognizable, and intangible. It moves uninvited and uncomfortably through my whole body. It does not seem to disappear, but rather feels like it is slightly increasing. A feeling like many times before; a huge pressure across the chest. A pressure that literally squeezes the breath out of me. This time, however, this pressure feels even more intense. And it is very persistent. And the pressure across my chest does not disappear even though I move from room to room, faster and faster. My breathing is very quick, I am gasping for breath, panting.

Something with an incredible and yet terrifying power is stirring within. As though I have an unpredictable and unreliable volcano stirring inside. A raging volcano about to have an eruption. *Something* deep within me that is stirring, moving and it's about to burst, to explode, and I don't know what it is. What I do know is that it scares the living daylights out of me.

Or maybe it's more like the thick massive wall of an icy cold tsunami that is about to overflow me fiercely and uncontrollably, drowning me from within. Maybe a combination of both. I'm afraid of this incredible powerful but very unknown raw force within. It's like a force of nature residing within me, just waiting to create death and destruction in its own way. I am afraid I will die because it is going to kill me. I am also afraid to feel it, to live with it. I am so afraid of this "force of nature". This indescribable 'something' within me that I do not understand, nor recognize but which I can feel moving deep within. Like a dragon that moves in its dungeon.

I have to do something. I have to go out. To get away, run away and escape this enormous raw power that is so unfamiliar and so threatening. Maybe if I keep moving around, I will keep this under control and keep it away from me? I am in a great hurry to get out. It's very cold but clear and crisp outside. The sun shines from the clear blue winter sky and the light snowflakes gently stick to my eyelashes. The brightness from the clear blue sky and all the reflective white snow that surrounds me, makes the snow crystals sparkle like diamonds. They make my eyes squint.

I walk quite fast. I can hear the squeaking and crunching sound from my shoes as I walk in the white snow. My footprints are the only visible footprints in the white snow. I go down to the ocean. It is very quiet and very still. The snow lies in drifts on the ground and on the trees. It makes everything seem even more quiet. Like the sounds are muted and muffled. It is very peaceful and very quiet. I can actually hear the soothing sound of the silence. It is almost as if I can touch it. The only sounds I hear are my own quick breaths and my feet that creak in the snow wherever I go. I meet not a single person. It's just me out there in the forest by the ocean. I am all by myself. The pressure across the chest is again very noticeable. Maybe it will disappear if I go a little faster or if I burn more calories? I must burn some calories now. I know exactly just how many calories I burn over a mile. I walk even faster for a while. I can feel some drops of sweat running down my spine. I walk like this for quite a long time. Perception of both time and space - as well as the sounds just fade away in the silence and stillness around me. The pressure over the chest still remains noticeable but has for the moment decreased slightly. Good, it's working. I have managed once again to escape from the unknown. Then, as I walk in silence in the quiet and peaceful forest, I hear a low signal from my cell phone. I take the phone out of my pocket and I see that there is a message from one of my closest friends. She knows that I am all by myself at Ingarö to rest.

I read the screen:

I Love You.

Simple as that. Nothing more. Nothing less than *'I Love You'*. The sharp pressure across the chest comes back in a renewed and intensified form. It's like a knife stab in my heart. It makes me flinch and I delete the message. I am just on my way to put the cell phone back into my pocket again when, once more, I hear that low signal from the phone. It's from my friend again. I open my cellphone with cold and stiff fingers and read *'I Love You'* again. It is something unfamiliar, something very unknown and scary that moves within me. It moves so fast. Frighteningly fast. This something, this movement, makes me afraid and I quickly erase the message to once again speed up my pace. To get away from this thing that is quickly moving and growing inside, coming from great depths. Once again, this low signal from the cell phone makes itself heard. Reluctantly I pick it up. It could be from my husband or family, so I pick it up. It´s from my friend again. I read on the screen *'I Love You'* a third time.

Whatever it is - that unknown and frightening thing that is moving inside of me - it moves very fast now. It moves with such an intensity and velocity that I can´t contain it or control it any more. I can't suppress that thing, whatever it is, any longer. It´s like the fierce explosion from the volcano inside of me I have been trying to avoid for as long as I can remember. This thing is absolutely flooding through me. Overflowing me. Overwhelming me like a huge tidal wave. An uncontrollable tsunami. The stabbing feeling in my heart is so intense that my knees fold and I fall down on the path. I gasp for breath.

I fall down. I silently fall down in the snow with my hands grasped tightly over my heart trying to prevent it from bursting or exploding. I remember that my fall to the ground is slow, very slow. As if I am falling in slow motion. It's like the ground is coming to meet me, approaching me, rather than the other way around. It´s not me being the one who has fallen down to the ground. It seems like I fall slowly into the snow, while holding my hands tightly over the heart, as if to prevent the massive pain that cuts like stab wounds straight into my heart. It´s my pathetic attempt to stick together in one piece. I try to hold onto myself, contain myself and not to break into a million pieces. It´s like I am holding on to life itself.

The pain, and its intensity, cuts through to my heart. The pain is excruciating and unbearable. Ice floes explode into a thousand sharp ice crystals and they cut deeply into my inside with their cold and razor-sharp edges. Never before have I experienced such intense, cutting and violent pain. It hurts so bad. An indescribable, unmanageable, intense and choking pain. In the middle of the chest. Right in the heart. I think I'm going to die from myocardial infarction. I remember thinking about my beloved children when I fall slowly and silently onto the snow. I am terrified and I am all alone and *scared to death*. The snow feels cold underneath me at first, but I hardly notice it because it feels like my whole being is on fire. Shattered. I am being shattered and I break into a million pieces and I burn up at the same time.

I am lying crouched on the side in the fetal position in the snow. Trying to keep myself together, trying to prevent me from breaking. Holding onto myself. Holding onto Life. My breathing is non-existent. Then this *something* that moves in my inner realm suddenly bursts. It cuts me down and finally explodes. It shatters me. I break. Something inside of me snaps, and breaks. It´s almost audible. I do not understand what is happening to me, I do not recognize it. This *something* that is pouring and overflowing within me. It is like a deep hidden well inside of me. There is no protection against it. There is no holding back. There is no help available.

Then hot tears are flowing down over my cheeks. They are streaming, pouring, flooding from a deep source, a deep well I didn´t even know existed. Salty hot tears running down my cheeks into my mouth. Suddenly, I hear somebody making horrible howling sounds close by. Who is screaming so heartbreakingly? The howls are like terrified ice-cold screams, petrified screams. A fear beyond words. Insignificant, and wordless. Bottomless, furious screams that echo in the otherwise silent forest. I flinch when I hear them. It takes me a little while before I realize that these horrifying primal screams are my own. But it's like the howling comes from a long distance away - far from within.

The fury of the primal screams penetrates right through me. It is not possible to protect myself from these horrible sounds. They, like the warm tears on my cheeks, just pour out of me. They are unstoppable, wordless, endless. I'm terrified beyond words. My heart is tightly held in the iceberg's cold and hard grip. I remain in the fetal position with my hands tightly clasped over my heart and I finally surrender to the power and intensity of the tears and screams. There is nothing I can do to prevent them from coming. I cannot suppress them or make them go away. There is nowhere else to go. Nowhere to escape. There is no-one who can help me.

I'm all alone in the snowpack with the pain and the scream that cuts like a knife through me.

The scream that cuts through the forest's snow-covered silence. The screams and the howls are like a furious primordial force. A primeval force that since ancient times has been deep within me - hidden for a very, very long time. It completely takes over everything like a furious and wild river that flows through me which cannot be stopped. A force whose fierce intensity I have never before experienced and which I do not understand. What is it and where does it come from? I don't recognize my own voice and I have never before heard anything similar to these sounds that are coming from me.

I lie crawled up in the fetal position for a very long time. A very long time. I can hear how my screams change intensity and also change in expression. How the screaming and howling sometimes take a short break and then they start again with renewed intensity as they suddenly increase in volume with new kinds of screams. Wild. High. Terrified. Beyond words.

Noises, screams and sounds like moaning. Panting. Groaning. Sighing. Gasping. There is something animalistic in the noises, something wild and raw in the sounds coming from my lips. And yet there is something almost magically free and liberating in all that crazy wildness. I am gagging, choking and throwing up, but nothing comes up. I am hardly aware of how the shadows grow longer or when the daylight is replaced by dusk and darkness. I am not aware of the cold and the dampness from the snow I am lying upon. Finally, the horrible screams diminish and are replaced by silent sighs and soft shakings throughout my body. Then my whole-body trembles, and shakes. The tears eventually stop flooding. They flow slower and slower so that, after a while, they stop by themselves. After a while, the sighs and shakings also end by themselves.

It gets very quiet. Unbelievably quiet. Deafeningly silent. I lie in the echo of all the screaming. I am surrounded by a complete silence. The silence is so obvious that I can almost feel it. It is so quiet that I hear light snowflakes falling against the trees. I hear some small animals moving around. Far away a dog is barking. My sense of hearing seems sharpened after all that screaming and howling. I'm lying completely still, like I am paralyzed for a while in the compact silence that surrounds me. Slowly I become aware that it is dark now. Quiet and dark. Very quiet. Very dark. Not dangerously quiet, nor dangerously dark, but more restful. Like a peaceful darkness. Perception of time has completely ceased.

Slowly, I now also become aware of the cold and the dampness from the snow that has long ago penetrated the clothes that coldly cling to my body. I move myself slowly and unsteadily to my feet. My legs feel shaky and wobbly like overcooked spaghetti. I have to lean against a tree. Feel the support of the tree. I feel completely exhausted. Exhausted and pumped out. Leached. Like being exposed to extremely hard physical exercise for a very long time. And yet in some funny and unusual way I am calm and still. I feel calm in a way I haven't felt in a very, very long time. If ever. Calm, as after a natural disaster that has passed and left. Not left with a trail of devastation but with a quiet sense of calmness. A calmness that reaches all the way into the soul. A calmness that fills my entire being, my whole being, which feels incredible and powerful in all that calmness.

The pressure over the chest - the feeling of being stuck in a tight and hard vice is completely gone. Rather, it is a feeling of something else, slightly larger. Almost like an expansion in the chest, in the heart. It is so silent in my head. My head is extremely empty, still and quiet and it is completely free from thoughts. I am amazed by this. I have never experienced something similar to this before. I like the unfamiliar silence very much. The silence has some kind of light to it. My anxiety and panic are also completely gone. They have vanished. There's not even an echo left of it.

My whole body shakes softly. It moves and trembles like a dry leaf in the wind. My body feels heavy and empty in an unexpected and good way. All I feel is calmness and quietness within. And the light that comes with the silence. It feels like all my senses are enhanced and strengthened. I can discern different shades of darkness, different shapes, and shades. I can hear the sounds of a bird's wing. I hear the sound of my own slow breaths very clearly. I do not really understand what has happened, but I feel that it is something new, big and unknown. A revelation of some sort. It feels of great importance in my inner realm.

There has been a huge shift and a shade of change inside. Something completely new and unknown I have never experienced before. Instead of the pressure over the chest and the usual worry and panic, I feel something else that I can best describe as P E A C E. It's brand new to me. Feeling this peaceful calmness. A kind of calm P E A C E F U L N E S S. Power, expansion and peaceful calm in the heart. It is so S T I L L. I also become aware that my breathing feels calm and deep. I don't even have to make an effort to breathe. How is it even possible? I can´t even remember the last time my breathing was this deep.

I stand still for a while, in the dark and silent forest and wait until my legs stop shaking. Waiting for them to carry me. I lean towards a tree as if it were my fixed point in life. My support in life. Then I slowly start to walk with my legs still shaking. I move slowly in the winter evening with the feeling that I have just been involved in something huge. Something vital and life-saving. Something indescribable. Again, it is like a revelation. A shift of some sort. I do not know and do not understand what it is, and I cannot really grasp it. I can´t pinpoint what it is. But I do know instinctively, I understand, and I just know, that it is something of great importance. Something new and something extremely crucial to me in my life.

Hardships often prepare ordinary people
for extraordinary destiny.
C.S Lewis

Red Glow

It takes me some time to finally come home to the house. My clothes are all wet and icy, closely clinging to my body. Everything is wet and cold. I am searching for the key. I hope I didn't lose it while I was lying in the snowpack. However, I gratefully find the key far down in a pocket, fumbling a bit with my icy cold and stiff fingers trying to open the lock before I can enter. I enter the hallway into the silence and warmth. It is quite dark in the house, but I welcome the warm and soft darkness and choose not to turn the lights on. It is so pleasantly still and quiet. I can only hear the sounds from the house that crack a bit in the wind - and the windows that are squeaking.

Without taking my clothes off I go straight into the sauna to turn it on. I drop all of my icy cold and wet clothes in a little pile on the floor and I allow myself to become one with the warm welcoming darkness inside the bathroom. I sit down in the shower and set the water at its warmest. The warm, beautifully warm water rinsing over me. The warm water that streams over my whole body. It feels like the heat from the shower also rinses through my interior with its warm flow. The soothing sounds of the water splashing down on the floor are mesmerizing. For a long time, I just sit in the shower and allow the water to flow over my body. It's like time has ceased to exist. It's just dark, warm and smooth. It is almost like being enclosed in a warm and safe uterus.

After some time, I move from the shower into the sauna, still without turning any lights on. My eyes seem to prefer the softness of the darkness that surrounds me. I stretch out my naked body on the warm bench and just lie still for a long time, enjoying the heat, the silence and the darkness. The only things that are visible are the glowing stones from the sauna. I let the heat in the sauna enclose me, and "tuck" me in. It is dark, warm and quiet. I am enjoying the unfamiliar and unusual tingling bodily sensations, the feelings of silence and peacefulness, but also the total lack of thoughts in the head for the first time ever. Although I have been in the cold and wet snow for a long time, I do not really feel cold. I am not freezing. Rather, it is like an inner heat like a "chill" - but soft and hot instead of a cold chill. Like a burning fever. It is as if there is a warm, soft and slow flowing red glow inside of me. The red glow is floating, moving like lava throughout my body. It is a very pleasurable feeling. The red glow flows slowly up and down my body and it warms me from the inside out, while the heat from the sauna warms me from the outside in. It is quiet, warm and comfortable in my body as well as inside the sauna. I notice that my breathing is still very calm and very slow, as in the aftermath of all the screaming in the snow. This too is also very new and unusual to me.

The rest of the evening I spend tightly wrapped in a woolen blanket in the old rocking chair that I´ve pulled up to the window. And I am just sitting in the silence. I sit comfortably in silence, in the embracing darkness, rocking and looking out over the snow-covered yard. I am content just to be there, without *doing* anything. I just look at the soft beautiful snowflakes falling down from the cloudy sky. I listen deeply to the soft crackling and crunching from the fireplace. The soft red glow is the only thing that illuminates the otherwise dark room. I am thinking of the kids, so I put on the cellphone and I call home to say I love them. I am happy to hear their soft childish, innocent and happy voices. After talking to them for a little while, I tell them that I love them and then I turn my cell phone off. Retreating into silence. Into myself.

I enjoy the silence. I actually enjoy being by myself. I enjoy the silence and the feeling of not having to do anything else than to just sit here in the rocking chair, wrapped in the blanket. I feel nice and warm inside and it is still surprisingly silent in my head. My mind is still free from thoughts. It is as if the thoughts no longer fit inside my head and instead there is an unexpected and inexplicable stillness and silence. All I experience is stillness, peace and quiet. And for the first time ever, that I can remember, I do not feel alone. Not alone at all. Just calm and still. Silent. Peaceful. Quiet. With myself. Somehow in myself. Within myself.

So, the darkness shall be the light, and the stillness the dancing.
T.S Eliot

23 years old,
already full
of self-doubt
and feeling
disconnected.

Ok (Lagom)

For as long as I can remember, I have had a huge need for approval from others - and also a huge need for 'fitting in'. An enormous need and un urge to be acknowledged, to be seen, confirmed, and to be well-liked. By everybody, all the time. Both as a child and in my whole life as an adult. One time, when I was a very young kid, the day care staff apparently called home to my parents to ask if I was getting any love at home. Because I always wanted to sit on their laps, being close to them and needing acknowledgement and confirmation. All the time I needed to be close to the staff working at the preschool. My mother has subsequently told me that she was offended by that conversation. And I can totally understand that.

I also have many memories of feeling 'fat' at the age of four. When I went to kindergarten (as it was called then) I told my daytime friends that I was fat, and I asked them if they thought I was fat too. I always held my breath when I waited for the judgement in their response. There was a guy I kind of innocently liked at kindergarten (at the age of four). He was calm and kind, not like the other loud and wild boys. He was one year older than me, and I wanted to become friends with him. At one point, I found some courage and told him that it was a 'fat girl' who liked him. He just looked at me with blankness in his eyes when I told him it was me who liked him. "Ok" is all he said and then continued playing and driving his toy car. Even though this was decades ago I still remember how stupid and rejected I felt at four years old. I thought that I was being rejected because I was fat.

I would stand in front of mirrors for a long time, and looked at what I saw (already there, already then, so young, so innocent) with self-criticism in my eyes and pinching my stomach. Wishing my body to be better, thinner, skinnier. I found it really awkward and difficult to be naked in the sauna at home with the family and to go to swimming pools. I didn't understand it then and I didn't show it, but I thought it was very difficult. I started to feel ashamed about my body at a very young age. Trying to take control over it, to be "in charge". I used to pull my stomach in and hold my breath when I needed to show myself naked. Or when I would swim in a swimsuit. It started at an early age, and soon became an automatically invasive behavior. To hold my breath and to hold my stomach in. To always be on the alert.

I also started at an early age to ask people in my close surroundings if I was 'just right' or 'ok', - the Swedish word for this is "lagom". I asked if my body was ok and if I was normal in my body. Was I accepted as me? The word 'lagom' actually goes back all the way to the Vikings, where they shared a pint of mead. Everybody was just allowed one sip so it would be enough for everybody. Nothing more, nothing less, just barely enough for everybody. So 'lagom' means sort of "around the team" but its meaning comes from lack, from scarcity and not abundance. Like, you cannot drink or ask for too much (of love, food, money, flow, anything). Because that means that others will be without! You are only allowed as much as everybody else, and it is deep in our Swedish imprints in our cells. And most of us are totally unaware of it, unconsciously.

During this decade I have come to understand, and realized, that "the illusion of scarcity, and the illusion of lack", unconsciously or not, has had a huge impact on how we look upon ourselves and others, and life in general. It is very deep rooted in our cells and in our genes, in Sweden. When I understood that and dealt with the emotions accumulated and connected to this inheritance, I was able to transform this into something that serves me better.

However, all my questioning and behavior; "Am I ok"? etc. towards my surroundings continued well into adulthood. Over the years, I have worn out many ears, and relationships both with boyfriends and friends, with this question. As I have already mentioned, it was very important for me to be 'lagom'. Not to be fat, not to be chubby, not to be too much or too little of anything in general - and in my appearance in particular. It was important to me not to stand out in any way - just to just blend in. And it became increasingly important. Being fat was "ugly", something that was not good. I just wanted to be "ok and approved of", I wanted to be seen, liked and included like everyone else, maybe just with another strategy.

After some time, I learned how to compensate for what I understood far later in life was self-contempt and a non-existent low self-esteem, by always being "the good girl". "Good and Sweet". It was also an important thing for me to be sweet. As well as Cute. I was "a good girl when I learned to read at the age of four or five. I was "good" at swimming. I was a "good" big sister. Whatever I was, or participated in, or did, I was "the good girl". So, I played the role of being "the good girl". I also became really "good at" being "the good girl" at school, to take responsibility, and also having responsibility for others. (In middle school I was simply being placed, without consent or approval, beside a guy who chewed on his disgusting foot warts and spat them out on my bench, on my schoolbooks, and on my stuff just because I was considered to be such a "good girl" and a responsible role model).

So, most of what I did in my activities I was "good" at. And, if I wasn't good enough in my own eyes then I quit that activity or that sport. Either I was 'good' and continued to be active in that activity or sport - even competing in it - or I was 'not good' and then I ended it.

The older I became, the more important it became to be seen as "the good girl" and to be "sweet and cute". I was under the illusion that I could hide the body that I was so ashamed of, and my low self-esteem behind playing many roles - such as being "good" and "sweet/cute". I actually thought that I could hide myself and suppress myself behind my many talents, roles or my sweet mask. No one noticed it anyway. At least nobody told me so. My inner experience though, was that I never felt good and sweet anywhere, or at anything. I could always be sweeter, more likable and better still. I was always somehow chasing that feeling, which of course always eluded me one way or another since *N O T H I N G* ever is permanent which I actually thought at the time.

There were many, many times that the thought hit me: "*If I am not the good girl, or the sweet one, then who am I? What am I then? If I am not that person, do I still have any right to live?*"

These thoughts, and everything that came with them, were so

breathtakingly painful that I quickly escaped them by pushing them away. I pressed them down and suppressed them. I simply pretended that they were not there. Like an ostrich sticking it´s head in the sand not wanting to see. While pushing the thoughts, and the feelings and everything that followed in the footsteps of the thoughts, down, I was constantly afraid of being revealed and shamed for being the fraud I felt I was. During certain periods of life, when needed, I also added the roles of playing "the good girl" and " the sweet/cute one" with being the "funny one". The girl who was playing around, telling jokes. Making people laugh. I was the one who invited and made jokes about myself and also others. The funny "joker". Obviously, I was very "good" at it.

In some situations, and with some people, I also played the role of the "skilled one". I played so many different roles. I was like a whole crazy choreographed theatre ensemble in one body. I did everything to be seen, appreciated, approved, applauded and popular. To be included and to be well-liked by others. And to be liked by myself. I played all of these roles to avoid being outside, excluded, not being 'someone' and not having to be discovered as the big scam I was. Sometimes it was really hard keeping track of all the different roles in different settings and situations. I played all of the roles and all the different parts so well for such a long time, that I didn´t even notice that I had lost myself along the way. I didn´t even realize there was something to lose in the first place.

It was very rare, if ever, that I showed who I really was and what I really felt, or what I really thought about myself and my life. It never felt like someone was listening or was interested in my feelings or thoughts. It didn't´ feel like there was somebody who wanted to know how I was doing or how I really was feeling. It made me feel rejected, small and insignificant. So, it became a habit to suppress my inner self and my expressions and I was not even interested in listening to myself regarding what I experienced, thought or felt. My inner realm was chaotic, but I never let it show on the outside.

At times when I did try to express how I was feeling, or what I was thinking, I got the usual answer, "just swallow it", "it was not so bad" or "don´t let it get to you". Sometimes it could also be; "keep in mind that you are such a good / responsible / sweet girl / daughter / friend / sister". So of course, I did as I was told. I stuck to it. I simply swallowed my emotions and my expressions. I suppressed it so I didn´t have to experience it, face it, feel it or deal with it. I pretended that it didn´t exist in the first place; "If you don't express it, then it ceases to exist".

And in time, of course, I also became very good at holding back, suppressing the real me and my true expression. I became so good that I even fooled myself for a while (half my life). Because, as I mentioned before, what I felt and what I thought wasn't even important. I wasn't important.

Over the years I learned how to press down all the thoughts and feelings that existed but that were not allowed to be expressed in their true essence. They were "not allowed" to appear, or to be seen or heard. Because it made people feel uncomfortable. And I was terrified of being rejected. So, I just did as I was told to do. When I was playing all my different roles, I got a lot of praise and approval - then I finally became 'someone'.

I was included then.
I was ok.
I was 'lagom'.
I was seen and approved by others.
I was safe and I was being loved.

There were many times I thought that my reactions had to be really strange, unusual, weird and wrong for what had triggered those reactions were not so bad. Not dangerous at all actually. Very ordinary situations triggered this within me. It made me feel like I was crazy and stupid. This craziness was also needed to be protected and hidden away from others to see. It made me feel like an "alien", that didn´t belong in this world and I needed to keep that deeply hidden. From myself and from others. This feeling inside of being wrong, stupid and a fraud grew and grew over the years. I still managed somehow to contain all those different roles, those parts, and all the masks, because that was what others expected from me. It was what I expected of myself. And, of course, I became very, very good at hiding the feeling of being wrong, stupid and being a fraud. I became so good at hiding it that I could also hide it from myself for several decades. I rejected it all to protect myself, and I became very successful at rejection.

A rejection is nothing more than a necessary
step in the pursuit of success.
Bo Bennett

Party pooper

I also feel like I am the constant Party pooper. The urge to talk about it, share it, express it in its ugliness. As I never did then, but as I can do now.

I feel like an outsider. Excluded. Left by myself, from myself. A leftover.
Like I am a small defiant and grumpy kid.
A kid who wants to be a part of it all but not being able to, doesn't know how to be a part, how to be included.
I am that kind of kid who wants to tug somebody's hair to get the attention, so I too can be a part of you.
I feel fragile. Vulnerable. Naked.
As if I am turning away from you but I really want to turn inwards towards you. To come closer to you. I just don't know how.

- *How do I become like you?*
- *How do I turn inwards to you, to get closer to you?*
- *How do I get closer to myself?*

I am sad and the tears are running but I hide them away. Shield them away. Feels like a tsunami of tears that want to get out. I feel alone. Lonely. Turned away. Alone and defiant. "Wrong in a way, wrong of some sorts". Not like you. I also want to feel included, to be with you, a part of you. I want to belong. But instead I am excluding and extracting myself away from you. I'm low, sad, insecure and depressed. I am turning away from you, so you won't notice. I am afraid that you will never care, never understand, never let me in. It's better that I turn away from you first than you turn away from me. I can't bear it when you turn away from me. Alone and defiant, with a painful and silently screaming sorrow inside, I turn away and shield myself from you.

The most important cage you can free yourself from is the one in which you care what others think of you.
Author unknown

Three Errors

I am in ninth grade. We will have a test in math. I do not like math and do not think I can understand anything. It makes me feel bad about myself and that I am stupid. I still study as "the good girl" that I am - so I sit for hours, and struggle and get so confused by the texts that explain the math task. I make it harder than it is for sure. Losing patience with myself and cursing my own stupidity inside. That I do not understand anything. How stupid can I be? I am such an idiot, a loser.

When the day of the math test approaches my sleep is really poor and it's getting worse and worse each day. When the day of the math test is finally here, I feel very tired and I am unable to concentrate. I have a huge knot of pain in my stomach while doing the test. I do hope it went well anyway. I cross my fingers and hope it was ok.

A few days go by and I am nervously waiting for the answer. I bite on my nails during daytime and my sleep is restless and worried at night time. When I do get the test result back, I am incredibly disappointed with myself. I get very angry. I won't show my test result to my friends. I lie to their faces and I lie to myself about it. I walk home with a burning and painful sensation in the stomach of having failed. I have let myself, and others down. *I am a failure!* This thought runs over and over again in my head. *How bad I am, how stupid I am. I am a stupid worthless failure.* When I get home, I go into my room. I put the test on my bed and look at it while I start beating myself hard with clenched fists. Punching myself in the stomach and in my head. I hit myself as hard as I can. Over and over again. Because I deserve it. I feel very ashamed and angry with myself.

"Three errors. Three errors with that stupid math test. Stupid. Stupid. Stupid. I am so incredibly unbelievably stupid. Three errors...Oh my God. I am so stupid, such a failure".

I continue to hit myself hard in my head and my stomach while hot burning shameful tears start to run down my face. I don't cry over the physical pain that I am causing to myself, which actually is some kind of relief for my own disappointment - I cry due to my own frustration and my "big" failure to have made three errors in this test. I cry because I am a stupid failure. A fraud. A scam. A shameful scam. A piece of shit. Worthless.

I deserve the hard punishment that is serving me right. It serves me right due to my three errors. It serves me right because I'm so stupid. Not worthy of any mercy. The three errors on the math test is corrected with a red pen and it's red markings are teasing me. Every time I stop hitting myself and I look at it on the bed in front of me, I continue the punches to my head and my stomach. I continue until I can't bear it any more. Then I lay down on the bed all sweaty and with a panting breath next to the test whose red numbers remind me of my "big" failure - and it burns straight into my eyes. I crawl into a fetal position. My knuckles burn and my stomach and head throbs and hurts. I have a terrible headache. My burning tears are making the sheets soaking wet. I feel horrible inside. I am in pain and it feels like I am going to throw up. It serves me right because I had three errors in the test.

> *When you set these high expectations and goals on yourself, that has an effect on the psyche. Eventually it wears you down.*
> **Author unknown**

ULLIS KARLSSON

I don't think I want to be married to you anymore

My husband and I are searching for a house or a larger apartment to buy. We live in a large two-roomed apartment of 70 square meters in Stockholm. A larger place to live would be nice so the children can have their own rooms. We go to the bank, to get a "promise for a house loan". We put a lot of time and effort into searching and reading house ads and we are bringing the kids for house viewings during weekends. It is a long process. We borrow my dad's car so we can drive to the different house viewings. Sometimes my mom and dad are supporting us by taking care of the kids when we are looking for houses.

There will be many opportunities. We find a number of townhouses that we participate in bidding for over a period of time, but we are the "constant number two". However, we quickly notice that the starting price goes up far more than we can afford. But we are thinking that soon, it's probably going to be our turn. Soon we will find something that suits us both in terms of price and geography. So, we continue to search. We keep our hopes up. We don´t feel that we are in a hurry though it would be nice to find the right place for us.

I am still on sick leave, and my husband is on parental leave with our daughter. Everyday life rolls on and all is good. New houses are coming up for sale. New views. I continue to dream of a house with a small yard covered with grass where the kids can play, and I can have some raspberry bushes. One day, just after yet another house viewing, my husband says without warning and out of the blue: "I don't think I want to be married to you anymore. I can´t take it anymore. I don´t know how to handle you and your depression and all of this any longer …"

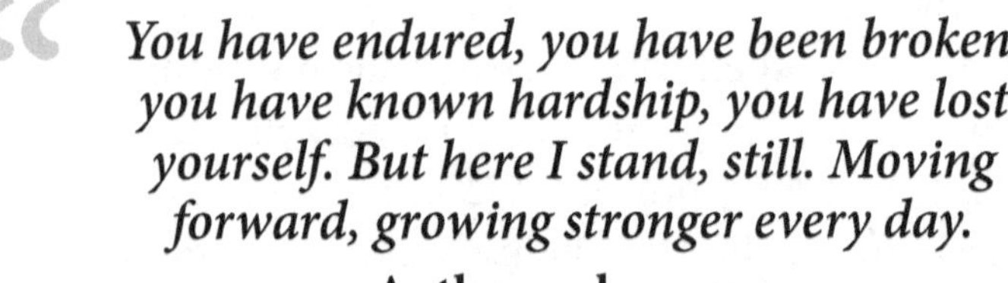

You have endured, you have been broken, you have known hardship, you have lost yourself. But here I stand, still. Moving forward, growing stronger every day.
Author unknown

The squeaking sounds from the stairs

My friend and I are maybe four-five years old. It is nice and warm outside in the middle of summer. Though it was so long ago, many decades ago, I clearly remember it with every detail; how it was on this hot summer day. Me and my friend are neighbors and we are at my place, in my room innocently playing "doctor". The 'doctors play' is that we examine each other's vaginas, with mirrors, feathers and with a toy stethoscope. The person being examined has taken off their clothes while the "doctor" is investigating. We take turns in exploring. It is exciting with this exploration. There is something "forbidden" about it and we play in silence. We play under my desk and the game is going on for a while.

Suddenly and without warning, the door is opened, and my mother enters my room. She looks at us and looks surprised, overwhelmed. My mother´s face is somehow contracted, and she gasps and holds her hands over her mouth. Her eyes are wide with an expression I don´t recognize. My mom looks straight at us where we are under the desk. She says nothing, just turns around and goes out and shuts at the door. I can hear how she walks up the stairs to the upper floor. Her steps are brisk and sound heavy on the stairs.

Our play, that for us was simply an explorative and innocent game was abruptly being interrupted. It quickly turned into something dirty and ugly that I couldn't explain. The play went from being just an innocent game to becoming something more serious and valued, something being judged. Somehow, I feel guilty and full of shame – yet, at the time, I cannot put my finger on it. I can´t really understand why this is happening and I don´t understand what is happening, but I feel it is a huge shift from something exciting and innocent into something bad. Something that feels heavy, disgusting and very shameful. Without words, beyond words, I just understand that we have done something completely and utterly wrong.

My friend and I look terrified and silently at each other. Our small fumbling fingers are trying to get dressed and hurry with the buttons. Then I hear loud steps from upstairs. The steps move quickly to the stairs. With horror, and as in slow motion, I can hear the squeaking sounds from the stairs. It is almost as I can feel how my room shakes in pace with the brisk and hard steps from the stairs. Oh no. It's my dad's steps. My father is coming. Mom must have told him that we were playing 'doctors'. I suddenly feel terrified and frozen inside. I am still fumbling with my clothes with my small nervous fumbling fingers. My fingers won´t obey me. They are frozen too and are moving too slowly. The squeaking sounds from the stairs are getting closer and closer. Every step is hammering, echoing inside of me. Time is running out. My father is getting closer, and I can tell from the sounds of his footsteps they aren´t happy.

I get all weak in my knees and spinning in front of my eyes. The thundering steps from the stairs fill my ears so I can't hear anything else. The sounds from the footsteps fill the whole of me. I try to hurry up with getting dressed even more. So does my friend.

I meet my friend's eyes again. We look with horror at each other, me and my friend. I can see that her eyes are shiny, and her lips are trembling. I feel bad and it feels like I'm going to throw up or poop myself. Or maybe both at the same time. I don't have time to think anything else before the door is thrown open with a loud and hard crash. My father enters in the doorway. He seems to fill up the whole doorframe. He looks me in the eyes and talks with a very calm and controlled voice, which at the time is even more frightening than if he had screamed at me.

"What are you doing?" he says.

"Nothing", I answer with a low and weak voice, as I look down at the floor. We are still half-naked and have not been able to get on our clothes back on. I look down at my toes, afraid to face my dad's ice-cold gaze.

"You know that what you are doing is bad. It is ugly and dangerous to do so."

No. I didn't know that before. But as my father says so, I can feel it so strong in my little body that is shaking from all the stress and tension. I know now that what we played, what we did was very bad, so very wrong. I feel ugly and dirty somehow. We were just playing a game where my friend was the doctor exploring my vagina and I explored hers. We didn´t know it was dangerous or bad before - but now my whole body feels both ugly and dirty on the inside.

This game, this day, and this memory really made a deep impact on me. A deep wound in my mind, my body and my soul. It made a deep wound on my sexuality and on the way I look at certain things. I have been carrying it around ever since. For decades. It created the memory of something ugly, something that is wrong, guilty and shameful and something that is forbidden. That there is something about me, and my body that is forbidden, ugly and wrong. You just don´t do that, it is as simple as that. And with hindsight, looking back, several decades later, this memory has affected my whole view of myself and my sexuality and relationships on so many different levels. It has affected my whole life much more than I could ever have imagined. That summer day so long ago when I, as a little curious and innocent girl, played the doctors game.

> *Shame is the most powerful, master emotion. It's the fear that we're not good enough.*
>
> **Brene Brown**

Like a shrimp on the floor

Days are passing by. It´s like they are all in a blur, in a grey fog, coming and going and I lose all track of time. Every day passing by in the river of life. My life is passing by, one day at a time. Nothing really matters anymore and keeping track of the days are not my priority. I am basically struggling for my life, trying to keep my head above the water.

So, it´s one day, just like any other day after the divorce. It´s still rather early in the morning and I have already been to the gym, pushing myself to the maximum to burn calories off. I am in this brief moment feeling some kind of "false" inner relief. Like a short break, a short escape from myself and my inner chaotic reality. The first round of cleaning the apartment is also already taken care of when it hits me like lightning. Just like that. Out of the blue. In this moment when I am actually feeling pretty good, and it sort of catches me off guard.

This excruciating pain that I felt once before, in the snowpack earlier this year where I was lying for hours. It is back with the same massive intensity. This horrific pain in my heart combined with absolute and complete fear and panic. This time it comes even faster than the time before. I freeze and don't know if I will survive this intense pain. Everything is suddenly spinning, and I fall down heavily, hurting my head while crashing hard onto the floor. I don't even notice it at the time.

I curl up in a fetus position, putting my arms around myself, trying to keep myself together and preventing myself from breaking apart or shattering into a million pieces. Alone again. I remember thinking, 'alone again' while lying like a shrimp on the floor. Then suddenly, just like that time in the snowpack not too long ago, I feel something deep within moving fast and wanting to burst inside. And that terrifies me even more. It's moving fast as a snake that is preparing to attack. It feels like a volcano that is about to explode. What's happening? Am I going to die here on the floor all by myself? And again, exactly as in the snow, it is impossible to contain it inside of me any longer. Hot burning tears are pouring down my cheeks, pouring as from a well, hidden deep within.

Muffled noises, grunts, moans, howling unfamiliar sounds and icy sharp screams. Like the ones from a petrified animal suddenly emerge and come out of my throat. Once again, also like that time in the snowpack, I am choking and throwing up. My jaws are opening so much so I can feel the pain in them. It feels like I am throwing up energy and puking up bad air and a sort of 'energy' from within. Nothing is visible but I feel it in my body. I don't understand it, but it's there, nevertheless.

My body is once again shivering and trembling as I am listening to these unfamiliar sounds from far away and from far within. I am still lying curled up like a shrimp on the floor. Then there is a feeling of immense grief, which is very unfamiliar to me - or has been inaccessible, undiscovered and unauthorized until now. And it hits me as hard as if I were in a car crash. The grief is overwhelming and it's hitting me hard in the chest like a compacted heavy and deep sorrow that I am not able to see or touch. The realization that I can't be with my kids as much as I used to. My grief is too heavy for me to carry and it feels as deep as an endless ocean.

I missed them so much. I longed so much to feel their presence and for their touch. To touch them, tuck them into sleep. I miss listening to their happy childish voices and their beautiful flowing laughter. I miss their beautiful innocent faces and their beautiful scent. The longing was so huge and so overwhelming. I miss them so much. So much. It was just like the whole divorce process. The separation from my beloved kids finally hit me. And it hit me rock hard. The insight that this was going to be my new reality, my reality of being without them for two weeks per month was killing me.

My heart was aching for my children. For so many years I had felt like I had failed them and let them down. That I had lost them forever. Not being enough for them, not giving them enough love. And that I also somehow, along the way, had lost myself. That I had failed myself too in many unspoken and unconscious ways. Like they were gone and that I was missing out on our everyday life together. And the longing was beyond words. The loneliness was hard as a rock, holding me tight in a very painful way.

I finally allowed myself to let go. I released all my grief and my feelings about the loss of my children and about my failed hopes and future plans. I also grieved and cried over my broken marriage. I was crying for what seemed like an eternity. Eventually, and gradually, the screaming and howling stopped though my tears were still running like a hot river down my cheeks. The grief now felt more like some soft waves after a storm. And, at last, the pain and the pressure in my chest was somewhat relieved.

I was still lying on the floor with soft shaking waves passing through my body. Still alone, when something again shifted. Suddenly, like that time in the snow, a strange and unexpected feeling of stillness came over me. A soft warm peaceful stillness - and it was both in my head and in my body. It was everywhere. It was like a voice or a whisper inside me but maybe even more of a feeling, or a knowing, from deep place within, that everything was eventually going to be ok. That all is well already. And that it will all somehow be well.

My body relaxed and became smooth and soft. The last remnants of the pain and the pressure in my chest vanished. I could hear the intense silence in the echo after all those different grunts and sounds and all of the screaming. It was as if I could somehow sense the echo. Like I could actually touch the echo. Being still in the echo - and from that place knowing that all is well, and all will be just fine.

I turned over onto my back. I became aware of the sunbeams flowing in through the rather dirty window, letting the sunbeams softly touch my skin. Feeling the sensation of warmth from the sun caressing my skin. Watching the leaves on the trees moving in the soft breeze and seeing how they were moving all the time. Soft constant moving; the leaves are not fighting against the wind but instead just following and flowing with the wind. As the wind comes and goes.

Easy, softly, smoothly. With no resistance at all, no effort at all. Beautifully moving, being totally free in and with the wind. And they also just know when it´s time to let go. To let go, fall, and surrender without holding onto something. One thought came floating to me on the soft river of stillness, while observing and melting into all this. "I wish I was like the leaves. I want to be like the leaves. I can be like the leaves. Maybe I am like the leaves."

Strength does not come from winning. Your struggles develop your strength. When you go through hardships and decide not to surrender, that is strength.
Arnold Schwarzenegger

The Preschool

My job. My job as a preschool teacher at a preschool. A job I so heartily have come to hate. Now, after several years, I have become very aware that I have never before been to a workplace with such a high degree of sick-leave employees - both short-term sick leave and long-term sick leave. I have never been to a workplace with so much stress and with such extremely dysfunctional ways of working, which in the long run is, of course, only a reflection of a dysfunctional management, organization and a dysfunctional non-sustainable approach.

It was a modern newly built preschool. A preschool where other preschools, or people who planned to start or build new preschools came to get inspiration on how an "open preschool" could be. Everyone who came was very impressed with the design and the architecture. It was so open, without all the different departments in traditional preschools.

I always thought when people came to visit us "they should really know what it is like to work here". This exemplary preschool with extremely high noise levels due to the dysfunctional structure. For me, who had already been on sick leave (for anxiety and sleep disorders at previous workplaces) this preschool, "the prison" as I called it, was a complete nightmare. My sound sensitivity was not helping me at all. It made my experience even worse in all this messy noise, with this loud and unorganized environment surrounding me. Large groups of children and intense sound with many high-pitched voices from children as well as adult voices. And noisy doors that were constantly opened and closed. It was pretty much chaos all the time.

I remember being so happy when I first got the job. I was handpicked by my boss. I had previously resigned as a physiotherapist from a retirement home, which also was like a "being a hostage", and completely dysfunctional in so many ways. At least from my perspective. So, getting this preschool teacher job and getting the opportunity to work with children was something I really looked forward to. It felt really fun and exciting. It had always been easy for me to get along with children. Children like me, it is as simple as that. And I liked them. So, my expectations were high, and I was really looking forward to starting work at the preschool.

It worked for a while as it was new and exciting and with many new colleagues in our large team. I made it work, even with spotting many flaws quite early on, as well as the lack of structure. After a while though, when the excitement of this new job had settled, it gradually became more difficult and harder to find any genuine inspiration and joy in the everyday tasks at the preschool. Moreover, when the tasks were not clear: 'what to do' and 'why' – it was always combined with stress. I wasn't sure of the role I should play or what was expected of me. It was very undefined and unclear. The change of my perception at work happened so gradually that I didn't actually notice it at first.

When I did notice it, it took me a long time before I realized that the workplace and the management were very dysfunctional in a lot of different ways. It was a very stressful job, with high intensity and a high volume of sound. Initially it was not possible to put your finger on what did not work or what it was that was making me unhappy. I often got sick and got caught by colds or the flu. I, who normally was very rarely sick.

At first, I put all the responsibility and blame on myself in regard to why it didn´t work the way it should. I needed to be the "good girl" that I had always been practicing becoming all my life.

I wasn't good enough.
I should make more effort.
I should just keep it together and be a little more capable, take even more responsibility.
Not to be so sensitive.
Not to bother, to care so much
I should be even more flexible.

Everyone else seemed to "succeed" and that somehow made me worse than the others because I did not fit in. I was ungrateful, for it was an important job that I had been hand-picked to do and I should be grateful that I even had a job.

I was partly employed to take care of the staff's wellness at the preschool. It didn´t take any genius to see that we in the staff were under a lot of pressure and that we were all stressed almost all of the time. Every week there were staff who were on sick leave and very rarely did we get a substitute. It meant that we were always short of staff. Big groups of children to manage and short on staff. At my first working year at the "prison", my experience was that one could count the days we were fully staffed on the fingers of one's hand. We were always told, "there is no budget for taking on substitutes". "There is no money". "You will manage." And, as loyal employees with the high empathy that many of us showed and with a desire to make a difference for the children who were our main responsibility, we "worked it out" somehow. But we barely managed and kept on struggling. Me included.

My perception was that there were no management that really heard that we needed substitutes for those who were on sick leave. We were talking about it, but nobody was listening. Although the people who were on sick leave changed, the absence due to illness was a constant factor and extremely evident. I often got ideas and came up with constructive proposals for management on how we could reduce stress and how we could improve our working environment. But, in my experience, there was no-one listening or having the slightest interest in changing the working conditions.

I remember that many of my colleagues often had a pain in the neck and shoulders and how I made the suggestion that everyone should come to me for ten minutes micro-rest and an easy neck and shoulder massage. This proposal was just waved away with the fact that there was no room for it. There was already a masseur within the unit at another place the employees could go to. Another suggestion from me was for a "Breathing, Yoga and Meditation" break for the staff for half an hour per week according to a circulating schedule, so everyone would be given the same opportunity. That proposal was also not acknowledged or listened to, as there was no opportunity or budget for it.

More and more people noticed that many of the staff didn't feel good. There were different groups within the group, and the managers made it quite obvious which ones were their favorites. Unfortunately, they also made it quite clear who did not belong to the favorites and I, of course, was in the second category. There was also a lot of talking about others behind their backs - "backstabbing" or "bullshit" if you prefer, out in the yard. The atmosphere often felt sour and bitter and we on the staff were worn out, tired, edgy, irritated and stressed. Days, weeks, and months came and went. There was no change for the better, rather, it was for the worse.

The sense of something I couldn't explain, or understand, something intangible, then slowly started to creep up on me. It was a very uncomfortable feeling as it made me shrink even more. It took me some time to become aware of it and to start to identify what it was. But when I finally identified it, I finally understood. I was being bullied by some of the staff and also by the management. A silent invisible bullying which in my experience was hard to see and acknowledge and hard to put a finger on. But it was very much felt and experienced. It felt like being left outside in the cold. My colleagues became silent when I entered the staff room, some even stood up and just left without a word. I was relocated within the preschool with no notice and for no reason, even though I was responsible, together with two other colleagues, for a specific child group. I never knew where I would be and could never plan or implement any planning since my experience was that I was "everywhere and nowhere" at once.

I got many of the most boring tasks that no one else wanted.

They changed my schedule without informing or checking with me first. I remember a particular staff meeting where we were in a rather large staff group and just before the meeting, we had talked out in the yard about what we had to address as we could no longer keep on working as before. What can the preschool do to help us and this stressful situation? And what was being done to decrease the constant sick leave? How could we work more with prevention at our preschool?

At the meeting I raised these points Suddenly, it was like everything we talked about in the yard was blown away. Colleagues stared down the floor or kept looking down at their finger nails. I received no support whatsoever from them. I felt so left out and alone. As if it was just my opinion and something I was raising out of the blue. All by myself, alone, I had to meet my bosses' contempt and dismissive gaze. Then, instead of talking about the staff's decreased health we spent almost one hour talking about where the bread baskets for the children would stand. And it was very important that we all liked and had an opinion about it. It was very important that we all joined this discussion. I felt very tired, exhausted, and very shameful after this meeting. I felt sad that once again I had done something inexplicable and incomprehensibly wrong. I made the mistake of expressing my opinion, my truth.

On one cold winters day I was asked to go out in the yard with 23 children, all under five years of age. All by myself, trying to dress 23 children with overalls, hats, gloves and boots on the small feet that did not always want to help. I was also alone in assisting them to the toilet visits before going out to the yard to play. I was so stressed and sweaty, both by the dressing and with the sound level of the 23 kids in the hallway. My colleagues sat inside and documented. There was a lot of time and energy spent on documentation, all according to regulations from the new law of curriculum.

This day, I would have to watch all these 23 children alone as parents came to collect them. A rather demanding mother came and wondered where her child was, while two small children were hanging on to me and pulled my arms. They were crying and freezing and cried that they wanted to go back inside. The mother got angry with me when I didn't really know where her child was, which is totally understandable since I was the one in charge of the children. Even though I had seen her child just a few minutes earlier, it was no guarantee that the child was still on the same spot since they are quite mobile at this age. I remember I was feeling very bad because of the mother's upset words towards me, and I was so ashamed, so I just wanted to collapse there and then over my failure of not being able to keep track of the children. I was putting even greater and heavy burdens of responsibility on myself. I obviously needed to become even better, and keep it together, even more.

After a full working week, I came home completely drained and exhausted and I just longed for the weekend and the time with my own children. Already after the Friday dinner, my "Sunday anxiety" knocked me over. The knowledge, the stress and the anxiety that I had to go back to work on Monday, slowly but continuously grew within me. The anxiety destroyed, and clearly poisoned my whole weekend and my time with my children. I never felt refreshed or well rested, and over time, this wore me out, drained me and burned me out. I became even more dissatisfied with myself, and with my life. I was angry, annoyed and moody almost all the time. I never took time for recovery and I didn't think anything was fun or meaningful any more. Despite this, I would go to work on Monday and think that I had a decent weekend and that it was still ok to get to work. But when I tapped in the door code and entered the preschool it was like the walls were falling in on me and the roof came down on me so that the space became narrower and unbearably heavy. My field of view became smaller and more and more narrowed. I felt imprisoned and tired before my work day had even begun.

I have been in therapy for many years and in various forms and one day, in therapy, I tell my therapist how I really feel without trying to hide it or diminish it. I tell her that I do not know how to cope. That nothing is fun, and it has been that way for a very, very long time. I tell her that everything in my life is mostly filled with anxiety, stress and worries. And I tell her that I do not know and do not feel the love of my children anymore. Of course, I *know* it is there, but *I just don't feel it anymore*. It was on this day that I finally let my guard down and with authenticity told her exactly how I feel and that I don't see the meaning of my life anymore.

"Having anxiety and depression is like being scared and drained at the same time. It's like falling into a bottomless black hole. It is like falling into the many layers of fear into the depth of the black inner hole that is eating you up from the inside."

She listens. She looks deep into my eyes with great concern

and says with a soft voice: "Ullis, you're really sick. Can´t you see it? You really need to be at home resting. This has gone too far now. I am afraid that something will happen to you."

Something does happen inside of me when she says this. First, I think, "Sick? I'm not sick, I don't feel that I'm sick, that I am having a cold, a flu or something." Then there's something in me that feels like a huge relief. My therapist has said that I can rest. So nice to get someone's permission, without asking for anything, just getting some rest. I have the permission to rest! It sounds so nice, and so easy - although there are so many different parts of me not even remembering how to rest anymore or what rest really is. When I rest, I go to the gym, or clean, or do something, anything.

My therapist has said that I can rest, and then maybe I can allow myself to rest. Maybe it's okay then? Being away from work for one week or so? It´s not that I like to be there anyway. I can rest for a week. "Okay" I finally say with some reluctant relief. "I can be on sick leave for a week. I can rest a week. I can do that."

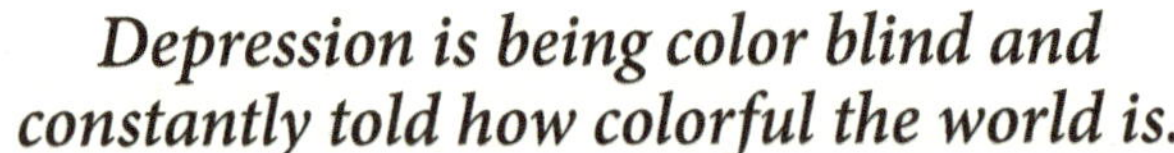 *Depression is being color blind and constantly told how colorful the world is.* 

Atticus

One sentence

One day, after one of my many long walks to keep the calories under control, I was in the food store buying groceries for dinner. I took a different way home and I found myself outside the library. I have always loved to read. I started to read from the milk boxes when I was four years old at the day care center where I was during the days when my parents were working. So, one day at home I just read the text out loud to my parents' surprise. When I grew up, I was always reading some book or other. It helped me to "escape" into other people´s lives and stories and I was always fascinated about people´s lives and stories. Reading was, for me, like one way of daydreaming of beautiful places far away and interesting and loving relationships. I never felt alone or separated when I was caught up in an interesting book. During my depression my cognitive abilities were so affected that I could not read at all. When I tried to read, I could read the same sentence over and over again and still wasn´t able to understand what I was reading. And even if I happened to understand the text, after reading one sentence for the 20th time, I forgot the meaning and the context it was in. So, I just could not grasp nor understand what the book was about. This was very disturbing, and it made me very sad.

So, this day when I was outside the library, I just went in without thinking. I had forgotten about the nice silence that is often found in a library. I really enjoyed the silence and sat down for a while just looking at all the books. Then I slowly moved into the aisles, touching the books and feeling them under my fingers.

All of a sudden, one book just fell off the bookshelf right in front of me, without anybody touching it. How odd that the book just fell off the shelf just like that, I thought. I picked up the book and started to look at it. I noticed, without paying too much attention, that the writer was a well-known Swedish Medium. So, without even reading the title I opened the book.

There was immediately one sentence that caught my attention. It caught my eye and when I read the sentence something touched me and moved me from deep inside. It was like that one sentence was actually talking to me. So, I went to the desk and the woman there helped me to get a free library card and I borrowed the book. It took me weeks and weeks to read, re-read and understand the book with my slow non-working cognitive ability. From that book two really important things emerged. Two things that were going to be lifechanging for me. I can see it so clearly now, when looking back in time.

The first life-changing thing was the one sentence, "Don't shop for love while you are grieving". The words I had first read in the library. When reading it again and again over the weeks I thought I understood it and it came to have a deeper meaning for me. For me it meant something like this; "Don't look for, or search for approval, love, confirmation, acknowledgement just in the outer reality, seek it in your inner reality and find it in yourself first. Give all of the things you are searching for or longing for to yourself first. From yourself. Fill yourself with the things you want, rather than looking for it outside yourself".

This whole idea, the whole concept was so new to me. It was

like a whole new way of thinking, so I just didn't get it at first. It was too big to take in. But it grew with me over time and gradually I came into a full understanding and it became vital and important for me. Just one sentence, but with such an important message. A message that was going to be life-changing for me. So, everything that I had always been looking for in my whole life in the outer world, was totally and completely missing in my inner world. All the love, security, safety, acknowledgement, approval, affirmation, the wanting to belong, all the connectedness, stillness, peacefulness - whatever that I had been looking for my whole life, just wasn't there in me.

Instead, it was just like an endless bottomless, painful and aching black hole inside. A hole filled with other things and other emotions, rather than any love and compassion for myself. From this dark bottomless hole within, the hole that I had unknowingly felt my entire life. For as long as I could remember. The deep scary inner hole I had always, unconsciously, tried to fill with something. Anything.

I tried to fix it with so many different things: trying to control my calories, and my weight by vacuum cleaning seven times per day, by exercising hard and intense, by drinking alcohol, by having - or not having - sex, by going to yet another course or traveling around the world. To always be busy. Busy. Busy. To keep myself occupied in every way possible. Constantly being in motion, constantly moving, striving, pushing, pressing and doing. Doing. Doing things all the time. Constantly being on the run, escaping or at least trying to escape from the pain. From the unknown and the unspoken. Always unconsciously and unknowingly fleeing from something that it was never possible to escape from. I was never really present. Never really here in the 'now'. Where ever I went, whatever I did, it was me all along, carrying this dark, empty lonely hole within me.

It was quite a shock to discover this. Like a very sharp, loud, painful and extremely unpleasant wake up call. It was like falling through the razor-sharp ice into the ice-cold lake. That everything that I longed for or searched for had actually never been out there. It was, and had always been within me. I had been looking in the wrong place, all this time.

The second thing I got from this book, was that this guy was doing some kind of 'Readings'. I didn't even know what it was at the time, but I instinctively knew that it was for me. Again, it was like the book was talking to me, and I just knew. With hindsight I know now it is clear that the universe assisted me, because his phone number was at the end of the book. So, I called him. It was in January 2008 and he was very busy, but I got an appointment with him in December 2008, nearly eleven months later. I remember that just by making this call, this booking, made me relax a little bit, like a small shift - a very subtle movement inside.

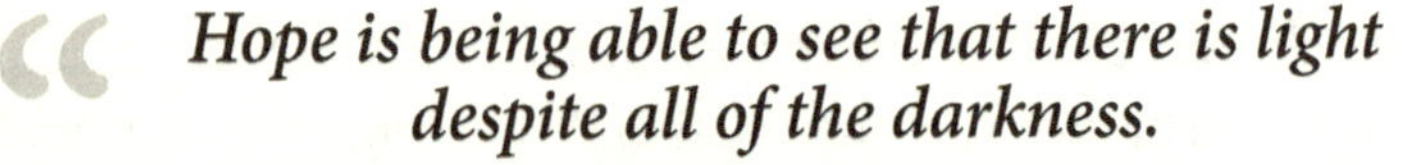

Hope is being able to see that there is light despite all of the darkness.

Desmond Tutu

You look very pale

One day when I am home alone, I get a mail from a friend of mine. She writes that she is going to a silent retreat for a full ten days. While I am reading this, something deep within me stirs softly. I don't know what it is, but it startles me a little bit and I feel curious about what it is, and where it comes from. It seems unfamiliar, not unpleasant at all, just more un-experienced. This "something" I experience is not like the usual thoughts that come into my mind, but from a totally different place within me. So, I call my friend and ask her about this retreat. She tells me about it and all of the sudden I find myself visiting the retreat web page. And then to my own surprise, I call them to talk. While the phone is ringing, I remember myself thinking, "This is stupid. Of course, nobody is there now to answer the phone. Why am I even doing this?". I hear the ringing and echoing into the empty air and then just when I am ready to hang up the phone thinking no-one is there - somebody picks up the phone at the other end.

I was so startled I couldn't say anything at first. Then I opened my mouth feeling stiff and awkward and introduced myself and we slowly started to talk. After 15 minutes or so I hang up the phone, look at it and wonder "What just happened?" With a lady's help I had filled out a form on the website and signed up for a ten-day retreat of total silence. I didn't know or understand why I did it at all. That night I told my husband what I had done and that I was going to a "silent retreat" for ten days, and that I really didn't understand why I had signed up in the first place. He just said "Okay".

The weeks went by and the retreat was coming closer and I got more and more nervous about it for some unknown reason. I don't know how many times I thought to myself that "I am not going. I have changed my mind and I will just cancel it. No big deal. I want to be home with my family and this retreat is not for me anyway." But I never cancelled, I never picked up the phone, never made that call or wrote that mail. It was as though I was waiting for it to disappear by itself. Which it never did of course.

Finally, the start day for the retreat came around. I managed to get a ride in a car with some unknown people from Estonia who were also heading to the retreat. The retreat had an "advertising board" on their website where one could ask for shared rides. My nervousness is thick and dense, almost as if I can touch it and feel it. It´s somehow very tangible. I am nervous for no real or obvious reason at all. At least the reason is not yet known to me. I ask the people in the car a lot of questions because they have all been to the retreat before, several times. The retreat place I am going to is a ten day "Vipassana Retreat" here in Sweden (a Buddhist retreat) which means "To see things as they really are".

The closer we get to the retreat venue, 250 km south of Stockholm, the more silent the other four people in the car become. It really scares me and freaks me out. Just like that. There is something about this rather abrupt silence that scares the shit out of me. The fear hits me in my stomach. It´s getting hard to breathe and to keep my eyes focused. A weird and sharp tone is ringing in my ears and I feel a cold shiver through my whole body. I fall into silence too, more as an attempt to contain myself and to prevent myself from opening the door and just jumping out of the car. It´s like I am "frozen" from this fear rather than wishing to be silent.

When we finally park at the parking space in front of the house and the driver turns off the engine it is deadly silent in the car, except from that accelerating sharp tone in my ears. I collect my bags and notice that my legs are all wobbly, like overcooked spaghetti. I stumble and walk on my way to the registration counter. A man is sitting behind the desk and he asks me to sit down, which I gratefully do. Actually, it is more like I am falling down onto the chair or slumping into it since my legs aren´t carrying me anymore. He asks me to hand over my phone, my credit cards and my keys while that sharp, loud noise in my ears turns up the volume even more. The knot in my stomach is now actually physically painful.

Then a thought hits me with the intensity of lightning, "My God it´s a sect. I have come to a sect. I am now in a sect. They are going to rob me and take all my money - everything I have and then maybe they are going to murder me while I am asleep. And they have my keys, and my home address and maybe they will drive there and…

"I must get out of here. I must get out of here. I must get out of here."

The man in front of me is looking at me with great concern in his eyes. He says something. I don't know what he says, but through my very narrow tunnel vision I can see his lips moving as though in slow motion. He says something again. Looking at me. Suddenly he takes my cold hand and his words become noticeable all of a sudden, and I understand what he is saying.

"Are you okay?"
"What?"
When I manage to answer him, my own voice sounds blurred, muffled, and like it's coming from a very long distance.
"Are you ok? You look very pale. Can I get you a glass of water?"
I am slowly nodding since I can't answer him back.

These hours, from my arrival to when we were given the information about the house rules and regulations, are really wrapped up in a grey, numb, fog. I don't remember anything. I don't recall what I did or if I was inside or outside the house or if I was talking to somebody. I don't remember anything. Nothing. It was like I was sleep walking. Totally paralyzed. Not knowing what to do or where to go. I just wanted to go home so badly. After some hours, during the group information, I slowly came back to myself, to my body and to my senses. It felt as if I had been somewhere else, in another place, in another world or even in another galaxy. I felt like I had been travelling for a long time, far away. I am so tired. So very tired. Exhausted. Drained. And also, very scared.

After the information sharing it is time for each and every one of us to get shown to our own seats and for the retreat to actually start. I find myself in a long line of unknown women and unfamiliar faces. We are all standing in a long row on the stairs. A long, long row of women of all ages, from all over the world. Being separated from men for the next ten days, who I guessed were standing in a row like this somewhere else. Because in this retreat, which is more like a monastery rather than a retreat, men and women are being separated for the whole retreat. I hear the names of these many women being called, and one by one they leave the line and go into the meditation room. My name is one of the last to be called because I am sitting close to the wall on a chair. The others are sitting on cushions on the floor. I have special permission to sit on a chair due to the pain and stiffness in my joints, mainly in my knee joints where I have no cartilage left. I can´t even sit on the floor due to my pain.

There is nothing more to do. Nowhere left to go. No more excuses. No more distractions, or activities. No more doing. No more acting. No more roles to play. No more escaping. The time has finally come to stop running, and to stop fighting. To stop running from myself, from this present moment. To stop running from life itself. And to stop "fighting myself" about the present moment. Time has finally caught up with me.

- *To do things differently.*
- *It´s time for change.*
- *A life changing change.*
- *It´s a matter of life and death for me.*
- *To be able to live.*
- *Or to just give in and to die.*

This thought hits me like lightning. As I realize this, I sigh loudly and find myself surrendering to the insight that the time has come to meet myself as I slowly place myself on the hard chair that will be my place from 4.30 AM - 21.00 PM for the next ten days.

> **When you think you have died and find yourself buried in a dark place, you are actually a seed planted in the dark soil ready to grow anew.**
> **Author unknown**

Laser sharp ice-blue coldness

At 4:00am, in the morning, they wake us up with bells. Nobody is talking. I live in a room with three or four other girls. I don't really know how many we are in the room since we are not allowed to have eye contact. I haven´t slept at all because some of the other girls were snoring very loud all night and I feel very tired and heavy. I get dressed and go to the toilet. My feet are taking me slowly and with a huge resistance to my spot in the meditation room. The bells ring again at 4:30am and it´s time to start day one. Last night we received a recorded introduction and an instruction on how to meditate during the first day. They told us just to follow the simple instructions. I sit uncomfortably as I look around to see that everyone already has their eyes closed and have already started to meditate. I close my eyes too and then sit and wait for something to happen. When nothing happens, I sigh deeply and start to meditate according to the given instructions.

After just a minute or so I open my eyes just to see that everybody still has their eyes closed. I feel restless already so move around on the chair a little, wondering for the 100th time since I got here yesterday what I have got myself into - and why. The following ten days weren´t exactly a "walk in the park". Something strange happened with regard to 'time'. Time somehow seemed to stretch out longer than usual and went so slowly, so, so, slowly - like in a very old film moving in slow motion. One minute felt like hours. Every evening we got a small recorded lecture on what we had done during the day and why, and then we got new instructions for the following day. I was tired and had a lot of pain in my body. I felt restless and uneasy. I was also slightly irritated all the time and I was also very hungry. So hungry. I was actually hungry for the whole ten days.

One day, we were told to add a new practice to the meditation. To sit completely still for one hour. When I say completely still, I mean completely still. If my nose was itching I wasn't allowed to itch it. If I had pain somewhere, I was to sit still with the pain and 'in the pain'. I was not supposed to flicker, to change posture or to move a single muscle at all. A couple of minutes into the meditation I am thinking to myself "Oh, I get this. This is easy, I understand it. I know what to do". Then without any warning I feel this massive intense pain straight in my heart that is like a *lazer-sharp ice-blue coldness*. It feels like my heart is clamped in a very tight vice, and the pain is so bad that I gasp for breath. I am still sitting straight on my chair, but actually it feels like my knees are stitched to my chin, like I am double-folded in my chair. I am really scared by now, thinking that I am having a heart attack and that I am about to die while still sat in silence on my chair, surrounded by my fellow meditators. Nobody would even notice that I was dead until after the retreat was over.

Then the weirdest thing happens; it feels like I am "zooming out" of the room and that everything is shrinking. And everything in me is shrinking too. My whole body somehow "disappears". My breathing diminishes into almost 'nothingness' but my senses get sharper and all I experience is that enduring and excruciating intense pain that feels like a lazer-sharp ice-blue coldness in and around my heart. But I still sit with the pain, without moving, holding my breath, waiting to die at any moment.

Suddenly, the bells are ringing that the hour is over and that it's time for a short and silent break. Still feeling the sharp blue coldness and that my heart is tightly clamped in the vice, I move slowly, and walk on unsteady legs to the meditation teacher to ask some questions: "What is this, what is going on within me?" She repeats as an answer: "I don't know. Something has probably been stored in your body and is just manifesting as pain right now."

"Will I die from it?" I ask.
"Most likely not."
"How long will the pain go on?"
"I don't know."
"What do I do?"
"Nothing. Just be with it and breathe. As it comes. As it goes. Don't judge it or criticize it. Don't change it. Just breathe. Just breathe. Stay with it and breathe."

So, I do as she says. Over and over and over again. Until the pain decreases slowly to be gone completely after a couple of hours. Leaving me feeling quite surprised, very relieved and extremely grateful that I didn't die in silence sitting on that chair. I lie in my bed, and I miss my children immensely. I cry a bit but this time I am not afraid of my tears; not afraid of this feeling. This night I sleep like a log for the first time in a very, very, very long time.

> *Your pain is the breaking of your shell that encloses your understanding.*
> **Khalil Gibran**

Free Flow

One evening, the recorded instruction is to 'observe' and to feel the free flow in the body.

The morning after, when I meditate, I don´t even know what it means. Free flow? What is it? How do I do it? Observe it? I sit with this all day being more and more frustrated and impatient.

Nothing happens, at least not the things I am expecting. I get very disappointed with myself.

That night I wake up from something, but I don't know what. But suddenly I know what it is that awoke me because I feel it. Everywhere. Inside of me. It´s an unfamiliar soft warm inner flowing and glowing, moving freely in me. It feels like a moving volcanic red lava flowing softly. That's exactly how it feels, and I am stunned and amazed - and the sensations are also amazing. I feel fantastic. I quietly ask myself in my mind, is this the 'free flow' that they talked about in the recorded instruction?

"Yes."

The answer comes from within. Then I direct my attention to different parts of my body, and I start to observe it, explore it, "play" with it. I feel the free flow feeling everywhere in the body - wherever I put my intention. And, what´s more, I can even change the 'quality' of the flow from the warm, soft, red glowing lava slow flow to the quality of water in many different shapes and forms. Water like an enormous wild and flowing river. Like the mighty Amazon shifting into to a fresh and playful mountain stream and then the intensity of a waterfall and the vastness of the everchanging ocean. I am exploring, playing and observing my free flow for the rest of the night. In the morning I am not even tired, even though I hadn´t really slept. Actually, I feel very energized and calm at the same time. Happy and refreshed and also curious what the day might bring. The echo of the free flow was with me all day.

The ebb and flow of daily life can lead to wonderful highs, crushing lows, and everything in between.

Julie Foudy

In the Echo of my Retreat

Here I am. In the echo of my retreat. On the other side of 'something else'. At this moment, I am feeling vulnerable, insecure, raw, naked. Yet there is also some kind of "strong and still" feeling deep within me.

- *Silent and sad.*
- *A bit scared.*
- *What is going on?*
- *An aching heart!*
- *Aching from opening and the longing to open even more.*
- *A longing soul*
- *Longing for Something. Everything. Nothing.*
- *Who am I?*
- *What am I doing here?*
- *What do I want?*
- *What do I need?*
- *What´s my path?*
- *What´s my purpose?*
- *What am I passionate about?*
- *How can I serve others?*
- *What shall I do?*
- *And how shall I do this?*
- *What is that is dying inside of me?*
- *What is the new that´s wants to be born?*
- *What do I need to see? To feel? To know?*
- *And why do I need to see? To feel? To know?*

Old fears and habits resisting the new 'longings', new dreams, new habits. New life emerging. Like a snake shedding its skin. Dualities. Two sides of the coin.

Doubt and clarity.
Fear and love.
Pain and pleasure.
Insecurity and security.
Illusions. Illusions of the old and visions. Visions of the new.
Not knowing and knowing it is okay not to know.
Resistance and stillness.

And then I allow the mystery of the unknown to unfold in its own way, in its own time. I allow the veils of illusions to uncover in their own way, in their own time. I allow and I surrender to this moment. It is what it is.

Relaxing.
Releasing.
Receiving.
Allowing!

Letting go and trusting the Divinity of the Universe.

All is well.
And this too shall pass!
Thank You!

> *Always say Yes to the present moment. Surrender to what is. Say yes to life - and see how life starts suddenly to start working for you rather than against you.*
> **Eckhardt Tolle**

PART 2

You are through the worst

When I look back to that day in the library such a long time ago, in the winter of 2008, where the book just fell off a shelf right in front of me, I realize now that this was an important turning point for me. I have always, somehow, been led to or guided to where I am today. Of course, I was totally unaware of this guidance back then.

After reading this book, with many "aha moments", I had found the courage to call the phone number that was at the end of the book. In the text it said that the author, besides being an author, was also a medium - a channel for information. This caught my eye and something rather unfamiliar, a tingling feeling, stirred deep inside of me. I called him in January 2008, and I can still remember how I liked his warm soft voice with an accent from the south of Sweden. It was a rather quick call and I got an appointment in December 2008, nearly eleven months later. During this period of time with a long wait many things happened in my life. And they were not all pleasant things. There was a lot of suffering, misery and pain awaiting me in 2008. Things "in transition". Luckily, I didn´t know what was waiting for me in the future.

My grandfather died and a very close, and beloved, friend of mine "broke up" with me. She just couldn't stand to see me so low, tired and depressed all the time. So, she broke all contact between us. It was devastating for me since she had been a longtime support for me as well as someone to "lean on".

Then one day my husband tells me that he no longer wanted to be married to me any longer. It came as a complete and total shock to me. After that horrible, shocking announcement we continued to live together for three to four months, which was one of the most painful times in my whole life, not knowing anything about my life or my future. How would it be to be separated from him? My partner and my lover for 13 years? And, being separated from my beloved children? Where would I live and how would I manage, since I was home on sick leave with depression and not much money? What would happen to me? To us?

This was all very stressful for me and it made me really scared. I repeatedly saw horrible vivid images in which I sat dirty, scabious and penniless. All by myself, playing the violin in the tube station. And then the Swedish welfare and social system would take my children away from me since I wasn't a good mother and couldn't provide for them. Who would ever or could ever, love me again, since I was "discarded and worn out"? How would it even be possible for anybody to love me? I didn't even love myself. On the contrary.

First of all, I don't even play the violin! And secondly, our welfare is really good here in Sweden, so I could provide for my children even though I was on sick leave, depressed and home from work for so many years! So, it didn't make any sense at all. I actually understood that it didn't make sense logically. Nevertheless, to me, it all felt very real at the time. And I was petrified 24 hours a day because of these horrifying images.

A decade later I can see so clearly how my mind worked at the time. It was always so negative, and so intense. The Buddhists call this "the monkey mind". Our mind that is constantly moving, constantly making loud noises that seem to be real. All the many illusions I had, about myself, and others and how life was supposed to be. All my limiting beliefs, and expectations, and how they kept me trapped, imprisoned in a cage, all the time. They kept me suppressed. Depressed. Unable to see things clearly. Unable to live free from fear. Unable to be grateful or happy. Unable to feel anything but negativity, hopelessness and despair.

My mindset, at the time, was always based on worries, fears and scarcity. And I always believed every thought I was thinking. It made me so scared and paralyzed as if I were "frozen". It was as though I was imprisoned by myself. I was both the prisoner and the "gate keeper" and stuck in this horrible, harsh, cold, lonely and painful reality. My mind, and my thoughts, were always imagining the worst-case scenarios and expecting catastrophes in every situation. Twenty-four seven. It´s not like that now of course, but still sometimes when I get scared my autopilot reaction from the past pulls me back into this catastrophic thinking.

When I finally met the medium after those rather turbulent eleven months, I felt really nervous and a bit awkward. But when he greeted me, and shook my hand, I could feel the warmness of his hand. When my eyes met his, I saw that his eyes were friendly and soft, and it was like he could see right through me. I felt both embarrassed, ashamed and safe at the same time as I sat down opposite him.

He asked me my name. I asked whether he wanted my first name, my second name or my nickname. "That name which is most you", he answered. "Ullis", I replied. So, he tells me five keywords for each letter in my name that describe my personality: "You are very Goodhearted - Courageous – Credulous - Super Sensitive and Stubborn. You use these qualities in a very unique way - and in what have been a very challenging combination for you, But, eventually, these qualities will serve you - and our whole society very well."

He asks me what I do for a living. Tells me that it feels like I have two different kind of jobs with two totally different energies: "It's strange, one job feels so dysfunctional and stressed, and noisy with many, bitter, competitive women. And the other one is a very important job, in silence from your heart, and where you make big and important decisions for many people also in silence, beyond words." I knew instantly what he was talking about of course and I nod and tell him what I do for a living. He nods too, patting me on my hand.

He talks about my life and how it´s been. He talks about my children and their personalities, and it´s so spot on that I am gasping. He also describes my ex-husband and the color of his eyes so it´s almost unbelievable how much he sees and knows. I have no idea how he could know all this, but it´s so accurate that I get goosebumps. He then looks straight into my eyes again and I can see a flicker of something in his eyes. Empathy mixed with horror? Love mixed with understanding? I don't know, but it feels like I am shrinking a bit in my chair and I feel quite awkward.

"Oh my God, so much pain! There is so much pain and hardship you have experienced in your life. But not all of it has been yours. You have been carrying around other people's pain and hardship too," he says. "Don't worry! You are through the worst now. Now it´s only the backwater left. You are home safe. All is well and all will be fine."

When he says this something bursts deep within, like a deep hidden well and my eyes start to fill with warm tears. Then he starts to talk about my future. And then a complete, new thought enters my mind from nowhere. If he could see all this; if he could know all this that has been in the past, even the colors of my ex-husband eyes, then what if he can also see what lies ahead of me, in my future, in my life! What if he can see what´s coming? What if...?

Twenty minutes later, after the session, this feeling inside of me that was bursting deep within is still waiting to be fully expressed. I find a beautiful church nearby. It´s empty and very silent. Candles are burning on the altar spreading a comforting soft light. So, I sit down and finally allow the releasing of all the feelings inside to flow freely.

It´s so very intense. My body is shaking, twisting and moving. I sob loudly and I gasp for breath between all the sobbing. What seem like endless warm tears flow down my cheeks and I am holding my hands over my heart as I allow the full expression of gratitude to manifest. It explodes intensely - but yet still soft, warm but not burningly painful, in my heart and everywhere in my body. It´s so very intense. And warm. And so strong. And so powerful. And so breathtaking. And very unfamiliar. And so overwhelming!

The gratitude I am feeling is totally overwhelming, flowing as a strong powerful warm river, as his words echo through me deep within my bone marrow. "You are through the worst now. Now it´s only the backwater left. You are home safe. All is well, and all will be fine."

- *And I cry.*
- *And I cry.*
- *I cry warm tears of gratitude, a powerful river of gratitude.*
- *Grateful that I am here.*
- *Grateful that I am through the worst.*
- *Finally.*
- *Grateful that somebody could see and acknowledge what I had been carrying and feeling for such a long time.*
- *Grateful to be alive.*
- *Grateful to hear that all is well.*
- *Grateful to hear that all will be fine.*
- *So very G R A T E F U L!*
- *Feeling G R E A T -F U L!*

I sit like this for what seems to be a very long time. I have lost track of time and space, so I don't really know, and I don't really care. I sit until the sobbing stops, until the gasping stops, until the warm tears have dried on my cheeks. I sit in complete silence in the aftermath. In the echo of my inner tsunami. I sit with myself, in myself and by myself. But I don't feel lonely at all. I don't feel alone. I feel at peace, filled, whole, complete and G R E A T F U L.

When I finally leave, I feel so cleansed. So clean. I feel very calm, so warm and peaceful inside. It feels like I have run a marathon. Like I have died and been reborn. Like the river of gratitude has washed away all the grief, all the shame, all the guilt, all the self-hatred, all the negativity that had been accumulating for so many years. It feels like I have drowned and been miraculously and freshly brought back to life and safely arrived at a new shore. It feels like I have found a new haven. I feel empty and yet very alive. I feel tired, yet excited. I don't feel scared anymore. My legs are as wobbly as they were in the snowpack some time ago as I am leaving the church and walking as in slow motion.

"You are through the worst now. Now it´s only the backwater left. You are home safe. All is well, and all will be fine." With this warm sensation, and this new knowing echoing in my mind, body and soul I slowly start to walk home.

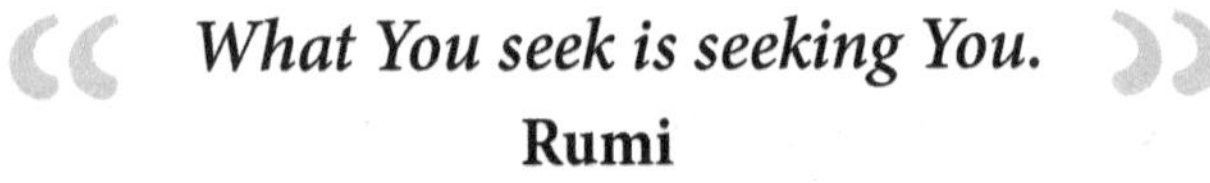

What You seek is seeking You.
Rumi

A Dead End

A couple of days after the reading from the medium, when everything was "same, same - but different", I go back to my job. The second I open the door it feels like the roof and the walls are closing in on me and my vision gets blurred and limited like tunnel vision. My breathing gets strained and shallow, and I am gasping for breath. I feel like a trapped animal. Then this thought hits me out of nowhere, "You are through the worst now. Now it´s only the backwater left. You are home safe. All is well, and all will be fine."

I just know what I have to do. I have known it for a while now, but have tried to suppress it, change it, sneak away from it, not listened to it or acknowledged it. Instead, I have tried to adapt even more at work. But now this insight hits me so hard and clear, so I can´t really escape from it anymore. I can´t struggle, suppress, deny, escape, adapt to or pretend I can´t hear it. I'm no longer trying to convince myself that I can´t see what is in front of me. I have finally reached a dead end.

The final dead end, where it is impossible to keep on going in the same direction or doing what I always have been doing and thinking the same thoughts I always have been thinking. The time has come to make new decisions, to take new actions, to change something. This moment is one of those times. I need to move on from the old, towards something new and unfamiliar. I need to change, to leave something behind so there is room for something else, to let something new into my life. There is something deep inside me which wants to go in new unexplored directions and in different ways and to find new paths. It´s now time for me to turn around and face it, whatever it is.

It is a turning point. I have come to see so many turning points in this journey of mine. And it´s funny that turning points sometimes happen gradually and so slow that you don´t even notice things changing - or that they are meaningful in the long run. But all of a sudden, something happens just in an instant that forever change your direction, your way, your path and of course, your whole life.

I know this is true. I know this is my turning point since I ran out of excuses a long time ago. Now I am also running out of energy, endurance and time as I realize that nobody is coming to rescue me. Nothing is going to be better by itself; I have waited long enough for that to happen. It´s time now to make a choice, make a move. I have to do something differently. I am the one who needs to take responsibility for myself and take action. So, I must turn around to face the point of no return. I have to resign from this job. I am the one who has to cut my economic life line. It´s all up to me. This insight comes from deep within and it´s frightening and scary as hell - but I know I have to do it. There is no turning back, no more excuses, no more escaping, no more struggling trying to adapt. No more nothing. I can´t teach about the Yogic philosophy to others in my yoga courses if I can't live it myself. I need to be true to myself. The time is now.

I need to let go. I need to jump from something familiar and safe that I know how to handle, however hard, boring, or draining it might be. I don't even know what it is or how to do it. How do I jump? What do I jump from? Where do I jump to? I need to resign from this job NOW. But how will I manage financially? I don't know, I haven't got a clue, but I do know that:

"I am through the worst now. Now it´s only the backwater left. I am home safe. All is well, and all will be fine."

With this in my mind I gather my courage, find my strength, connect with my breathing and shake loose the feeling that the roof and the walls are coming down on me. I blink a couple of times to clear my vision. And for the first time in countless days and many years I feel quite calm as I walk to my boss to say that I need to talk to her about something important.

> *The secret to Happiness is Freedom. And the secret to Freedom is Courage.*
> **Thucydides**

Keep life simple, keep it plain

That day in the hallway at work was one of many turning points for me on my long inner journey back to peace and simply finding myself. I realized that I wasn't going to be saved or rescued by anybody. Nobody could help me. There was nothing left for me to fix nor a puzzle that needed to be solved. My dream scenario was that it would all change for the better by itself, but it just hadn't occurred yet. So, I realized that if I wanted change then it was all up to me. That I had to rely upon myself.

" *If you want another result you need to change your recipe.*
Quote from my Instructor at the
Stress Rehabilitation program. "

So, I finished what has been the process of down-shifting from my work, which was a whole process in itself over time. I didn't even realize at the time that it was down-shifting I was doing. From full time, to part time, to half time until the day when I finally resigned from my work. I left on the spot and I have never looked back since. I left without even saying goodbye to my colleagues, even though I had given three months' notice when resigning. I went to my doctor and told her the way it was. That I couldn't put my foot there ever again, that it made me sick and panicky just thinking about going back. She knew my long journey with the long history of depression, panic attacks, stomach-ache, sleeping disorders and more. She looked me straight in the eye and I could see that she fully understood me. So, she picked up her pen and wrote a prescription that declared I was sick and was unable to work during the three months' notice I had at work. This allowed me to still have 80% of my income while I was home on sick leave. There are no words to describe the relief in my mind and my body. I was taken care of for three months. I had something to lean on for a while and I never had to go back to the job I hated so much. Somebody actually saw me and understood me.

I was so incredibly grateful that I cried out loud. I sat there for a long time with my doctor just crying and crying out of sheer relief. We held hands and looked at each other, and I could see the tears in her eyes too. I cried all the way home from the doctor, and I felt like I was 20 kilos lighter when the crying finally stopped.

The three months at home, after visiting the doctor, is still a "blur" for me. I don't remember what I did or if I did anything. I took long walks in nature. I rested a lot and curled up in a fetus position during the day time when my children were at daycare. I cried a lot. Other than that, I just can´t remember.

One day, after a long walk and a long rest, something very subtle and very quiet, manifested from somewhere deep within. Even though it was very subtle and very quiet, I could hear it so clearly. I could feel it vibrating through me. It's a deep, deep longing from a very unfamiliar, undiscovered and unconnected place in me and it startled me with its subtle quiet expression.

Several years later I came to understand that it was the deep longing of my soul that had been abandoned and neglected for such a long time. It cried softly: "I want to be free. I want to be at peace. I want to be happy. I want to love and to be loved. I want simplicity. I want to live my life more simply. I want to live my life plain." That moment my business name was born: 'Plain Yoga'. It was a reminder to myself and a dream for me to follow. "Keep life simple, keep it plain".

'Plain Yoga' has had a significant meaning for me over the years, both as a reminder of where I have been and what I have been missing out on for so many years. But also, what I am striving towards, dreaming of, moving into, longing for and what I also want to share with others and give to others. The deep longing from my soul for:

Freedom.
Peacefulness.
Happiness.
Love.
Simplicity.
"Keep life simple, keep it plain".

It's been with me every day since it came to me and, nowadays, I feel grateful that I get to share this with others in my work around the globe. My vision is simply to create a happier, softer, easier, juicier, more loving and divine world for us all to live in. And it all starts within me and within us all! I just didn't know this back then.

 *Keep life simple, keep it plain.* 

A longing of some sort

One day, not too long after that winter's day in 2008, when I fell down in the snow pack, I felt even more drained than usual. More exhausted than usual. I went for a massage and two hours of therapy and I also had a foot-bath before I went to bed that night as I was really tired. Surprisingly enough, and actually for some unknown reason, I dozed off. And I had a dream. A dream that was so different from my usual nightmares that it didn't feel like a dream at all. It was a vivid, soft and strong dream and it felt more like a vision. In this dream, this vision, I saw myself on my favorite cliff out in the archipelago, close to my parents' house and it felt like I was levitating. I did Yoga, but another kind of yoga than the physical kind of yoga I was used to. It was a softer, more gentle and tender slow flow. A very feminine - and yet very powerful kind of yoga. And it made me feel so good to be levitating in the dream. It was such a magical feeling. I was so at ease, so light and happy. I was both peaceful and full of peace! I slept really well that night.

Next morning, I got a mail from the friend that had texted me "I Love You" on the day I had fallen into the snow. There was a link in the mail. It said, "Yoga course for Stressed people" and it was a course to become a Yoga instructor. So, I contacted the man responsible for the course and asked him some questions. To my surprise, I ended up signing up for the course.

During this time, I was also participating in a 'Stress Rehabilitation Program', a course specially designed for a group of women in the same situation as I was in, with depression and burnout. One of the staff from the Stress Rehabilitation Program asked me a question: "If you could describe how you feel about yourself and your life using the metaphor of a bottle of soda, how does it feel for you now? I answered, "Well, it´s like a thick, disgusting, stinking black tar in a prison of thick indestructible glass".

As the weeks passed by on the Yoga course, and the Stress Rehabilitation Program, I started to notice how my "bottle with this black, stinking tar" started to transform from what was complete darkness into a more dark-grey shade with lighter grey stripes in it. And the glass wall seemed to become a bit "thinner" as well. I could feel a gentle shift in my body and in my mind, a gentle easing in me, that I wasn´t used to feeling.

At the end of the Yoga course, my teacher told me that there is one spot left for a one-and-a half year course to become a Yoga teacher and a Yoga therapist, starting right after the current course. He asks me if I want it. I feel something is stirring inside. A longing of some sort. And I hear myself answer: "Yes, but I don't have the money." "Well if you feel that this is what you want, and you decide to take the position, the money thing will solve itself," he answered.

So, I did sign up for this longer, deeper transformative inner journey of mine while totally clueless about what was awaiting me. And my teacher was right! Totally unexpectedly I received the exact amount back from an insurance policy related to my job. Money that I wasn't even aware that I was entitled to. So, out of the blue, the money issue solved itself in a way I had never expected or experienced before. I couldn't quite understand it and couldn't really grasp the magnitude of it. Today, I am very grateful for that opportunity and for what materialized as another turning point. I am also incredibly grateful for the direction of my inner journey that those one-and-a-half years took me on.

I allow the longing from my soul to be greater than my many fears!

Connection

I must admit that I was very curious and also, of course, very nervous about the course to become a Yoga teacher and Yoga therapist. It was very much a case of mixed emotions and quite a lot of resistance from my mind, such as excuses and circumstances for not participating. A lot of fears were moving in the "muddy waters." Anyway, years later, I can now see that it was not by chance that I was going to participate in this course. Actually, once again, and very unconsciously, I was guided by my soul and my higher self - even though I didn't realize it that back then.

When the course was about to start, I had a private two-hour session with my teacher. This turned out to be one of the biggest and most profound turning points in this inner transformative journey of mine. First there were many different questions, then he summarized them for me, explaining from the Yogic perspective, why I had all of these dysfunctional symptoms. He talked about why I was depressed and had a burnout and why I had sleeping disorders. He explained *why* my life had been such a struggle, such a battle and also *how* I could change this quite easily in myself! This was absolutely mind-blowing news to me. I have never heard anything like this before. I never knew anything like this. The insights, and the impact they had on me, were huge. Extraordinary. Enormous. Massive. Beyond words!

In an instant I saw my whole life, like pieces of a jigsaw puzzle being solved in ultra-rapid time. I saw how every tiny piece of the puzzle fell into a full picture, a whole picture. It was really simple actually. Simple - but not easy. But I knew. I just knew and I felt that this was a missing piece, *the* missing piece, the profound missing piece that I had been looking for my whole life. In everything I had done, everything I had experienced, everything I had longed for. And I had been searching for it all over the world, in many different forms, and in many different relationships. In various situations, shapes, sessions, courses and educations. I had searched everywhere in the outside world. And now, finally my long and arduous search was over. It was here. It was already inside of me. It always had been there, but I had lost it along the way and lost it through life. It was the one and only thing that made the difference for me, from the black hole to being whole, being and feeling the wholeness.

This vital piece of information had an important impact on me and my life. This lifechanging missing piece of information. But what was it? In the Yogic perspective it is all about *connection* and your environment when you enter this world. The connection with your mother and your father and your ancestors. Your "heritage from your lineages" and in what environment and society you grow up in.

Basically, not only are you inheriting the color of your eyes, hair, and skin – you are also inheriting your parent's behaviors, their imprints and their programs. You may even inherent their "frozen emotions" (emotions never shown or expressed). You have also inherited their ability - or inability - to show and express emotions including how to handle situations, how to react and how to act on your reactions. You do this on a very unconscious level. And *everything* that hasn´t been expressed or resolved, is stored deeply and unconsciously within you.

This means that unresolved pain, suffering, situations, issues, emotions, and traumas can be passed on for many generations until somebody - maybe you - decide to consciously work through them and thereby bring them into the "light of consciousness". And from there you start to transform them. Every change, every transformation, every personal growth starts with awareness, by becoming aware of something. You cannot change anything you are unaware of. If you are unconscious about it then you cannot change it.

Of course, I knew bits and pieces of this before, but not in this way, and not with this deep understanding, this deep knowledge. In a flash, I could see clearly why I had always felt so insecure and why my self-esteem (my value and who I am if I am not doing or performing) - had been so poor through my life. In other words, the reasons why I only felt worthy when I was doing something or performing in some way. I could also see that my many fears and worries were due to never being connected or grounded. I had never been fully here, never been fully present. I had always been somewhere else, on the move, in my past or in my expected future to be.

When I was a newborn baby, in the early 1970`s, there was advice from the Swedish Health Care system that you were only supposed to breast feed every 4th hour, and not "freely" at any time - like it is now. So, basically that meant that the baby couldn´t get what it needed, when needed. And also, even back then, Sweden had a very well developed and advanced day care system so the mothers could go back to their jobs really soon. Nowadays, we have one of the most beneficiary parental leave systems with 400 or something days per child, where we are given 80% of our income to be home with our children. This is all being paid for by the taxes we pay here in Sweden.

Anyway, I was left with a daycare mother for many, many hours a day when I was only three months old. Apparently, this did something to my connection with my parents and I developed the imprints of never feeling quite safe and secure, so I had to search for this outside of myself. I was always searching for "quick fixes", or for others approval, or wanting others to heal me. This "lack" of trust and connection had many different expressions and one of them was having this constant urge to be competitive or feeling the need to compare myself to others. By doing this, I always felt I wasn´t good enough. The feeling that I constantly needed to do things, to be busy, and always needing to perform in some way. Always escaping myself, searching for answers outside of me. According to the Yogic perspective, the lack of connection and the environment are two of the biggest causes for developing many of the imprints that might lead to symptoms that are common in western society, such as different kind of stress related diseases or burn-outs.

A poor connection can develop into low self-esteem as well as not feeling safe or secure. Not being or feeling grounded and not being fully connected to yourself or others. Just imagine how much pain and suffering this causes in our relationship with ourselves and of course with others. Just take a look at this world, as we know it today, with all kind of conflict going on around the globe. No wonder there has been so much pain and suffering in my life. Losing myself. Feeling lost. Not connected. The wound is due to the broken connection to myself and, as a consequence, also to others.

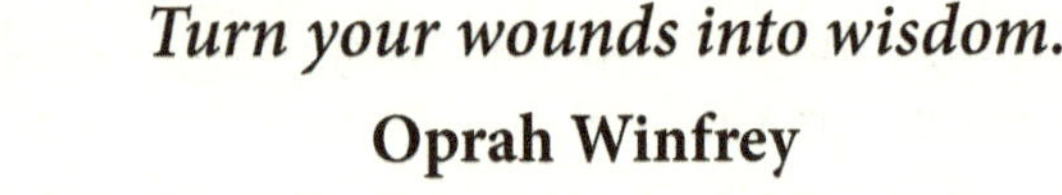

Turn your wounds into wisdom.
Oprah Winfrey

ANDEtag - Grab the Spirit

Today, with my new perspective, understanding and knowledge from my teacher, I am seeing the whole picture for the first time. I have also got to know some of the tools I needed to start to heal myself. And it´s so basic I could hardly believe it! So incredibly basic. Very simple, but not easy.

It´s all about breathing. It all starts with, and it all comes down to, our breathing - with our conscious breathing. It's about connecting with, and enhancing, our conscious breathing. The Swedish word for breath is "andetag", which literally means "grab the Spirit, get a hold of the spirit". We were all born into this world with a breath, connected with Spirit, and when it´s time for us to leave this world we also do it with a breath. That's when the Spirit leaves our body.

Whenever we are scared, frightened, nervous, sad, depressed, insecure, or not feeling safe it has an impact on us and also our breathing. Whenever we feel shame, guilt, self-loathing, hatred, anger, irritation, frustration, stressed, full of doubts or something similar, our body and soul, and our breathing is being contracted and constricted. It happens so subtly that we may not even feel it or notice it. It happens unconsciously.

When we feel love, balance, joy, happiness, harmony, peacefulness, pleasure, stillness, trust and connection to ourselves and others, our breathing slows down, and expands. So does our body and soul. We become one with Spirit. One with the breath, oneness. We become connected. Connected to ourselves and our inner reality. Connected to others and the outer reality. So, we can heal the broken connection with our parents and ourselves with our conscious breathing. When we connect with our breathing and our Spirit, we are talking about developing spirituality. A spiritual awakening, a spiritual growth starts to happen, and a higher consciousness occurs. When teaching spirituality, if it´s not embodied or connected with our breathing we lose something that is of fundamental importance for us and our clients' personal growth. For example, "mental spirituality" which is only one of many aspects of spirituality that doesn't go as deep as when it´s embodied.

I could write a whole book explaining what happens when we start to breathe properly and when we are starting to liberate ourselves through our breath. I have researched, explored and invested this huge and important topic for many years now - actually for more than a decade. The thing that I have discovered and witnessed, and I continue to witness every day, on the underground, in crowds, in hospitals, in yoga studios and everywhere else in society is that thousands of people are not breathing properly. Their breathing is inadequate. Constructed. Restricted. Limited.

> *Breathing is the first act of life, and the last. Our very life depends on it. Since we cannot live without breathing it is tragically deplorable to contemplate the millions and millions who have never mastered the art of correct breathing.*
>
> **Joseph Pilates**

Limited breathing always causes and creates a limited life and a limited spirit one way or another! If we look at a newborn baby, we can see the ebb and flow - and the easiness - of proper breathing. Then something happens to many of us as we grow up and we start to limit the breath and limit ourselves. We even lose the breath, meaning that we are losing ourselves on a deep and profound level. One of my many teachings, that comes from more than two decades of researching, exploring and investigating, both within myself, but also with others, is to provide the tools to connect to ourselves again. Connecting to our true essence. Connecting us with our heart. Connecting us with spirit. Connecting us with life itself. I often think of the quote "And the truth shall set you free." – from the Bible. To me it´s more like "And the breath shall set you free."

I took a deep breath and listened to the old bray of my heart: I am, I am, I am.

Sylvia Plath

Highly Sensitive Person (HSP)

In the winter of 2013, I found a new piece of the puzzle regarding understanding myself better. Understanding myself better has been an important part of my healing process. And when I understand who I am, and we all understand who we are, it is so much easier to love and to forgive ourselves and each other.

I am meeting a friend over a cup of tea at her place. We haven't seen each other for a while so we have a lot of catching up to do. She is telling me about some books she has been reading. One of them is about "Earth Angels" – angels as in human forms here on earth, also called "Lightworkers". They are people who are here to guide other human beings into more love and light and also an elevated consciousness. I personally think we need more of these Lightworkers in this world. If we could all be more responsible and take action for our own inner "garbage", we wouldn't treat ourselves, or others, or our home like we do today. We wouldn't dump our inner "garbage" on others, or in the environment. Because it all starts within. Every change, every improvement and every transformation, starts within us. My inside world is mirrored on my outside world.

Anyway, it was very interesting listening to my friend and her insights and reflections on those books. The other book she was reading was about Highly Sensitive People (HSP's). When she told me about it, it really resonated with me. Something stirred within me and I got goosebumps and chills all over my body. Deep within, all the way in my tailbone I felt a sensation as a soft movement of excitement. I became really curious and wanted to know more, so we 'googled' it. There was quite lot of information on this. There was even a test I could do to find out whether I was a 'highly sensitive person'. So, I took the test and it indicated that "my scores" were very high on the scale of being a highly sensitive person. I was actually rather shocked. And I was also inspired and interested to learn more about this.

I had never heard about it before, but when I read about this on the internet it was like reading about myself! Finding out about myself and knowing that there were others out there just like me was very revealing! After all these years I finally understood why I had always felt like an "alien". I had always felt that I was misunderstood and needed to adapt to the norm. Trying to be "normal", like everybody else. Not wanting to stand out. Always trying to adapt, to fit in. To belong and to be included. Not to express how I really felt. When I was reading all this, it explained a lot of my actions and reactions over the decades. I understood I had suppressed my emotions and my sensitivity as a pure survival strategy in order to cope. I had suppressed my intense feelings as some kind of protection for myself. It was such a huge revelation, and a huge relief for me to read about this, so I started to cry in the coffee shop out of pure happiness and gratefulness. Throughout my whole life I had felt that there was something seriously wrong with me. That I was stupid and crazy. Not like the others. And instead it turned out that I was just being sensitive. And, from what I read, this could also be a great gift if we know how to navigate our sensitivities. Over the years I have also come to understand that I have a highly sensitive personality and I am also an 'empath', having an introvert empath personality. There is a slight difference there.

Being HSP, I feel a lot of concern and empathy for others. And, as an empath, I can actually *feel* what others are feeling without even knowing this. This explains what the medium told me that day when he said; *"Oh my God, so much pain! So much pain and hardship you have experienced in your life. But not all of it has been yours, you have been carrying around other people's pain and hardship too. Don't you worry! You are through the worst now. Now it's only the backwater left. You are home safe. All is well, and all will be fine."*

Basically, I haven't just been carrying my own "garbage". I have also been carrying around others. No wonder it has been such a heavy burden for me to carry! Being both a HSP, and having an empath personality also explains why I don't like to go on public transport for example. If I enter the underground, or a bus, I feel everybody's accumulated and collected stress, pain and worries and it becomes dense and heavy in me. Or those many years at the pre-school where I could feel my colleagues' illnesses, depression, negativity and stress. This has really made me look upon myself with more understanding, acceptance, and more loving eyes. This understanding has made me softer and more forgiving towards myself - and also of others.

Today, I see that by being a HSP, and having an empath personality, is one of my greatest gifts. Now I know how I can use it instead of abusing it, in every part of my life. In my work this gift is an invaluable tool. With this gift comes a great Intuition of what others need to dissolve, their "frozen emotions". I merely become a "channel" and guide for love, wisdom and transformation. I am truly grateful for this important piece of my life puzzle. I don´t have to struggle with it or be "against it" anymore. I can actually flow with it.

I am sensitive. I love deeply. I think deeply about life. I am honest, loyal and true. I appreciate the simple things. I will not change or harden into this world. It is this sensitivity, perception, sincerity, awareness, affection and gentle grace that makes me who I am.

Author unknown

Forgiveness

One of the many ways I have found to 'retrieve myself' has been to work through and fully experience and feel all the emotions that have been deeply and unconsciously hidden in me. I call them "frozen emotions". Not easy at all. Not so nice. Not so comfortable. Not so smooth. Not exactly want I wanted or anticipated. And with much more resistance than I could possibly have known.

The phrase "face yours fears" is a lot easier to say than to actually do! But I did face them, tuned into them, felt them and thereby transformed them. I didn't really have a choice. It has been very necessary, rewarding and of great importance to me. It made the difference of dying or living, living or dying. The choice as to whether to continue with what I was doing or die! Or to do something differently and to live! Forty-eight years of suppressed emotions have now come to the surface. Layers and layers of accumulated, rigid "frozen emotions" have been acknowledged, accepted, dealt with, moved into and through, felt, experienced, embraced, processed and finally transformed. This transformation of my many layers of "frozen emotions" have brought me to where I am today.

Another aspect for me to feel, to work with and to work through has been:

Acceptance
Forgiveness
Compassion
Patience
Trust
Love.

I really must admit that none of them have been my strong or well-developed character qualities. They have never come naturally to me and I certainly didn't get it from my parents. So, during this inner journey, back home to myself, the Universe has kindly given me plenty of opportunities to practice each one of them.

Acceptance: For me, acceptance is easier to talk about than to actually feel. I mean, how do you accept things you don´t want? Things you don´t like? Things you didn´t expect to come in your way? Things you never asked for nor dreamed of? How do you accept things when you don't feel acceptance? I have always had a hard time and a lot of struggling just trying to accept things as they are. I always wanted to change something, both in myself but also in how I perceive the outer realm, the outer reality. I always wanted to change something about my body, my looks, my grades, my feelings - even my entire being. There was always something that could be better or improved. I never felt good enough. I always wanted fun things to happen. I always wanted the sun to shine. I hated it when it was cold and dark which it is five months of the year here in Sweden. I had such a struggle even trying to accept this, so I started to travel at an early age.

My unconscious behavior patterns have been both to escape and to fight or struggle. The 'fight or flight' response, from the reptilian brain. It all depends on the situation and how stressed I am as to what reaction emerges. But to say that it has been a lot of fighting, a lot of struggling that led to my burnout is not exactly an exaggeration. So, my personal growth this decade has also been about learning to accept what is. It is what it is. If I don´t know, then I don´t know. If I don´t like it, I have to like it that I don´t like it. As I said, the Universe has given me many possibilities to practice acceptance on a daily basis, in small things, as well as in big matters. It was extremely challenging for me to accept life itself. Today, I am grateful for all these lessons learned!

Compassion: This has been quite a challenge for me. I have always felt it so much easier to feel compassion towards others. That hard, rigid, abandoned part of me has been very resistant and reluctant in being compassionate with myself. And it has been easier the days when I feel good about myself, or when the sun is shining, or when I can give it to somebody else to "become something" - a rescuer, a hero, a good-hearted person for example. I am still practicing this. And the Universe has given, and still gives me, plenty of opportunities to practice compassion. I am grateful for this.

Patience: A lot easier said than done for me. My body type, according to Ayurveda - the traditional healing and knowledge of life from ancient India - is 'Pitta' which is the fire element. And yes, I do have a lot of fire in me. Fire as in a lot of passion, ambition, drive, energy, endurance, heat, power, strength and also stubbornness. For good and bad. My energy is naturally quite fast. And I am very fast in both my body and mind: taking actions, risks and judgements. My temper is "hot blooded", meaning that I have a lot of frustration and restlessness in me. I have always felt frustrated by people, things or situations that are "slow". Slow thinking and slow moving.

I never liked to wait for anybody or to wait for something, anything. When I needed to wait, I waited very impatiently and with a lot of frustration, whether I was waiting for people, in queues, or for things to happen. My whole life, I have been too good, the good girl again doing things to get appreciation from others and to be loved. To take over responsibility for myself and others. Which actually, is very disempowering for me, as well as for others! I always tried to take control over situations by trying to speed things up. By being a control freak. I got really stressed when I felt I was losing control. Having control is just an illusion in the first place and it´s based on fear. Just by hearing the word 'burnout', one can surely understand that there has been too much fire. Too much fire caused me to burn up and thus become burned out.

I have used, and abused my energy, my power, my fire, in the wrong direction, in the wrong way for me for a very long time. All this power of mine that was misdirected and abused for so many years. It was used to suppress, to control my emotions within myself in particular and life in general. To slow down, and to be patient, was of course very challenging for me, but also a very important part of the whole process. It started with my breathing and slowing down my own breathing gradually through the yoga that I developed for my own needs. This has now transmitted into everything I do - like downsizing my life or "down slowing my life."

Today, I still have a lot of fire, passion and power, but it´s much softer and more gentle. More of a feminine fire rather than masculine. And it's used - not abused - in a way and in a direction much more wisely and "ecological". I am not consumed by my fiery flames. As you might have guessed, I also was very untrained in feeling patience from my childhood. The Universe again nicely stepped in and gave me many challenges to practice patience by. Of course, we all get better at it when we are practicing regularly, on a daily basis. Again, I am grateful for my everyday practice.

Trust: The Swedish word for Trust is 'Tillit'. It is a palindrome, meaning that it is the same word spelt backwards. TilliT, is made of the word **till** in Swedish, that means "to". Not only that I need to trust something that is not there, I need to put my Trust *into* something, for something to change. This too was a hard nut to crack. If you have never felt safe and secure, never felt trust, it isn´t so easy to start. Like where do you start? And how? How does it even feel, to feel trust? I can see so clearly how this is so connected with not being or feeling connected. Not being grounded. Not to myself, to my body, to spirit or to my surroundings. My early unconscious imprint of not being connected has had a major impact on me, with the result of lacking trust (again coming from scarcity, fear based). Lacking trust in me, and trust to me. Trust in others, and to others. Trust in life, and also to life. Lacking a sense of being safe and secure within myself. It means that I was constantly worrying, and afraid for this or that. Never feeling, nor realizing or knowing that everything was going to be okay.

I used to have so many unconscious and non-understandable fears that ruled me and my life. They controlled me, without me even knowing it. Obviously, I needed to create some kind of protection for lacking trust. Being a control freak was one. Trying to control everything and from this space trying to create a false sense of trust. "I can do it by myself". And "I am alone". Again, being "the good girl." Everything is entangled in everything. Everything is connected with, and to, each other. Everything was connected with that I didn´t feel connected. It all came back to that, over and over again. I am still practicing trust every day. And again, I am very grateful for this practice! At least I *know* now, in my mind, that everything is okay and will continue to be so. I trust that I can lean into myself and into life. Even if I don't always feel it. There is a huge difference in just knowing.

Love: For me, I have never felt authentic and genuine love towards myself. And if I did feel love on some occasions, the love I felt was always conditional. I needed to earn it by doing something or by performing, to be "the good girl, the sweet girl, and the responsible girl". That I, as myself, and in myself wasn´t worthy to be loved. I have never experienced unconditional love towards myself if I haven´t been doing something to earn it. This too is a daily practice! To love myself without doing, just by being. Even if I am not "the good girl doing", if I am not competing, comparing, performing, even if I have gained weight – feeling and knowing that I am still lovable. That I am still worthy of being loved by myself and also being loved by others.

Of course, all of these aspects are connected to, and with, each other. Everything is linked and intertwined together into a "togetherness". Everything is entangled. Everything is connected. If we miss out on one of these aspects, we will most probably have other imbalances as well. If we balance and strengthen one of them, the other ones are also being balanced and strengthened. As I have originally come from a fear-based perspective, shifting it into a more loving perspective has been, and still is, of vital importance for me. It is an ongoing process. Both for myself personally on a micro-perspective level, but also for our society on a larger scale - the macro perspective. It is of vital importance for all of us to become more aware and enlightened by increasing our consciousness. It is only then we can make new choices, so we can change, move, and transform, both individually and also collectively, from a fear-based society and emerge into a more loving society. Increasing consciousness is what I do professionally for a living nowadays. It´s my job. This is one of my contributions to this world, one of my gifts. And I love it!

Finally, **Forgiveness:** Entangled with and connected with, everything else. Of course. The word forgiveness in Swedish, is **'Förlåtelse'**. I like both the English and the Swedish word. They have a slightly different meaning to them in a way that really resonates with me. För **<u>låt</u>** means that you **let** something happen to you. You allow something to happen. So, it´s a choice, where you can allow forgiveness to occur, or not! **Se**, in the word förlåtel **<u>se</u>** means **see**, I see, and therefore also allow forgiveness to occur. In the English word, 'For **give** ness', somebody is giving something, also allowing something to happen. Who is giving the 'for **give** ness'? You? Me? To whom? Who needs to be forgiven? In my case it has been me **giving,** as well as **allowing** the for **give** ness to myself, and also the forgiveness to others!

So, I am both the giver, giving forgiveness to myself and I am also the receiver, allowing myself to receive, to accept, to trust the forgiveness. Letting it happen. I have really needed that, and I have longed for forgiveness. This one might have been the hardest one to work with, to work through for me. This one, and also the love aspect. To forgive myself for all the suffering, all the pain, all the abuse I have inflicted on myself and put myself through.

To forgive all these years of self-loathing.
To forgive all the layers of self-hatred. All my disdain.
To forgive all the limiting thoughts that I had about myself, over the decades - my body, not being good enough nor beautiful enough.
To forgive myself from keeping a distance from myself and from others.
To forgive myself that I abandoned myself, and others, over and over again.
To forgive myself that I wanted to punish and hurt myself.
To forgive myself that I haven't been present for my children.
To forgive all the shame and the guilt and all the sorrow I created in myself.
To forgive myself that I wanted to end my life.

> *When you forgive, you change the past-and you sure do change the future.*
>
> **Author unknown**

For me, it has taken some time, but I have used my new allies, acceptance, patience, trust and a lot of compassion and love too. And I have given myself forgiveness and I am being for**given**! I have such a loving and compassionate and understanding heart, and my heart has for**given** me! Can you imagine? Forgiveness has been a very important piece of my path to personal growth, to expansion and to liberation. Forgiveness brings freedom. Freedom and empowerment.

> *I believe forgiveness is the best form of love in any relationship. It takes a strong person to say they are sorry and an even stronger person to forgive.*
> **Yolanda Hadid**

Connecting to something very deep and profound

It is spring 2015. Life is rather good. I feel healthy, my children seem to be fine, my relationships are good. I love my work, and what I do. Teaching yoga, and spreading consciousness gives me a sense of meaningfulness and a purpose. It makes me happy and content to see all the changes and transformations my teachings create in the lives of my participants.

Still, I am sensing, a rather vague feeling that I am sort of waiting for something to happen and longing for something else; something more in life. I am very familiar with this feeling, even if it isn't as intense, sharp and edgy as it has been before in my life. I don't feel to the same extent that I need "something", or "anything" to save me, to rescue me. Yet, it feels that something is "in the air" or moving beneath the surface. I am waiting for some un-defined "thing". I don't know what this might be or what it is I am waiting for - just this inner knowing that there are new layers to be explored. What more do I expect from life? When I was ill, I only had one wish; to be well and healthy again. Now that I am healthy, and my life is fairly good, I have many wishes and dreams.

One day, as I am scrolling and reading posts on Facebook, there is one post that immediately draws my attention. It is a retreat, a shamanic, spiritual and sexuality retreat, taking place for the first time in northern Europe. My reaction, just by reading about the retreat, is really interesting. I get both scared, anxious, out of breath, curious and feeling ashamed at the same time. So, with this information from my body, manifesting as these mixed emotions, I know I must go. I just know it. I feel it deep inside. My mind, and my ego makes up all kind of circumstances and excuses for not participating, but deep inside of me I feel I need to go. I feel the urge of participating. I have no idea why; all I know is that since it stirred up all kind of emotions in me, there is still a need for facing and also healing these emotions.

I am not telling my partner about the retreat straight away. I am having an inner dialogue, questioning whether or not I want to ask him to join me - or if I want to do this retreat by myself? After a couple of weeks, I decide to tell him that I want to go and that he can come along if he chooses. But I am going anyway. I need to go. He gets curious and decides to join. We sign up and pay and as the weeks pass by, the retreat is getting closer by the day.

When we finally arrive at the retreat, I am scared, nervous and anxious. I just want to escape from everything, I want to leave the place so badly that my legs hardly carry me as I walk to the venue. I can barely talk, because my teeth rattle so much in my dry, rigid and stiff mouth. My heart is pounding so hard and so fast in my chest. I feel cold sweat all over my body. And I wonder why I am putting myself through this over and over again? Participating in events, courses and education that really freaks me out and takes me way out of my comfort zone. Why? Why do I do this? What´s the purpose? What is pushing me towards stretching my limits all the time? The answer, and the insight, that comes is the same as many times before. I am being led by the purpose of my soul.

And I am being guided by my higher self. It is as simple as that. By now, I have come to know that my personal evolution occurs when I face all the things I fear, way outside of my comfort zone. This uncomfortable place is where my personal growth happens, where I am able to heal and liberate myself.

During the opening ceremony I become even more aware that this week isn´t going to be a "walk in the park". I sigh and surrender to my many emotions, letting them go in their truest essence, the way they want to express themselves. During the week we healed and processed a lot of 'frozen emotions, both as individuals and also for the collective, in the "field". When you are including shamanism, spirituality and sexuality, and integrate them through your body, you work on many different layers and many various aspects at the same time.

The whole week was very intense, from early morning until late at night. We did several ancient ceremonies, practices and exercises, to heal the feminine and the masculine parts that exist in all of us. Parts that have been abused, misused, rejected or neglected in many different shapes and forms. If there is an imbalance in one aspect it obviously affects and causes imbalance in another. Everything, every ceremony and exercise, aimed to heal and to align the sacred feminine with the masculine, into the sacred union. The sacred union, the alignment and the wholeness, in each and every one of us.

The last day, and the last ceremony, was dedicated to the celebration and healing of the wounded feminine. The men had their gathering, preparation and sharing for themselves in a room and the women had their gathering, preparation and sharing in another room. We, the women, were to receive yoni (yogic name for vagina) de-armoring, from the men. A woman's yoni, the essential source of life, contains a lot of stored, accumulated, conscious and unconscious stress, pain and unresolved traumas.

I was terrified. I was so nervous and worried. Not nervous like the other women who didn´t know who they were going to work with. I knew that I, luckily, was to receive from my beloved partner. But I was still nervous.

Nervous, that I was going to be in "performance mode".
Nervous, and ashamed about my body.
Nervous, that I was going "to fail" somehow. Fail him. Fail myself. Fail us in some way. Nervous, that I was going to compare myself with others, and their experience.
Nervous, that I wouldn´t stay present, that I was going to escape from the experience, escape from my body, mind and soul.
Nervous, of doing something wrong, being too much, or too little.
Nervous, of what was going to come to the surface and in what kind of expression.
I was really terrified… and so incredibly nervous.

Once we got started, all my fears vanished in a millisecond. My partner was so in tune with me. So loving, so gentle and I was being so present, so conscious and aware of every subtle sensation. Every touch and soft, loving caress from my partner. I was also very connected to my breathing. The ceremony lasted for some hours and I lost track of time. It was a very authentic ceremony, sensitive, yet powerful and truly beautiful. It was a magnificent and very vulnerable experience, a deep inner work, connecting my yoni with my heart. I was both touched and moved by the whole ceremony. A lot of old, conscious and unconscious, traumas and pain were being released. It was a true awakening from within. It was connecting to something very deep and profound, long lost, and something I had never experienced before - a deep connection with something bigger than myself. I would describe it as a pure connection with spirit, a spiritual awakening, in fact an 'enlightenment'.

After my yoni de-armoring, I was in my own "bubble" for several hours. I saw everything so clearly, every shade of the colors in nature were enhanced and so bright. I could see details I hadn´t seen before as well as the wholeness at the same time. I could hear each sound from nature so clearly separated and yet still united. All of my senses were clearly enhanced. My whole body was vibrating. I moved very slowly and consciously. I could feel every foot step, and the touch of my bare feet connected with, and deep rooted into, Mother Earth, Gaia. It felt like I was both levitating and being extremely grounded at the same time. It was impossible for me to move, or even to walk, fast. I could see that others were talking to me as I could see their mouths moving - but I didn´t register what they said. My yoni was pulsating, vibrating, awakened and in tune with every heartbeat. And I was filled with so much love. So much love like a bright flowing, radiating light that filled every cell within me. The wholeness of me. I had never experienced anything, even close to, being so beautiful before. I remained in this blissful state for hours.

> *"When we touch the place in our lives where sexuality and spirituality come together, we touch our wholeness and the fulness of our power, and at the same time our connection with a power larger than ourselves."*
>
> **Judith Piaskow**

This sexual and spiritual awakening has been a deeply profound piece in my puzzle and on my journey of retrieving myself. It created a whole new imprint on every level of my human and spiritual being - and my existence. It enabled my soul to realign with my Life Purpose. It completed '*The Journey Home to my Heart*'.

AFTERWORD

Freedom, Flow and Love in life

I am sitting here by my kitchen table, watching the low but beautiful December sun shining with its last long and lingering sunbeams, almost dreamlike, through my window. I sip my hot warm, sweet tea and I notice somewhat distractedly that my windows are really dirty when the last lingering sunbeams softly kisses my face and turns this day into early afternoon. A lazy thought enters my mind, "Maybe I should clean my windows?" I take another sip and feel the sweet tea fill my mouth and my nose with its scent. "No." Just like that from nowhere: "No." And I smile to myself feeling happy and at ease. "No, I am not going to clean my windows." Not today and probably not tomorrow.

And why? Because, I really don't care. Not at all really. And I smile again to myself. And most certainly not the way I used to, when all I was thinking was to keep it nice and clean all the time. That time almost eleven years ago, when cleaning the house was only one of my many ways and strategies to keep myself distracted. Always keeping myself busy by thinking and doing a lot of things, one activity or another. In my mind or in my body.

Being occupied, constantly, to keep the anxiety away. To keep the worries away. To keep the pain and the suffering away. To avoid feeling the fear. That time, not too long ago, when I could clean the house seven times a day. When I was constantly moving. Constantly on the move *to* something. Striving. Constantly on the move *from* something. Escaping. Constantly moving away from myself in any way possible.

I take another sip. Enjoying every sip. Enjoying every moment and no longer feeling that I need to do anything particular to be okay. To be worthy. Enjoying every slow conscious breath. I am enjoying watching the sun with its golden rays of light, kissing this day goodbye with a promise of coming back tomorrow maybe. Or some other day. Now, I have all the clarity I need within me, so it doesn't matter if my outer windows are dirty. Couldn't care less. I have more fun and interesting things to do. To be experienced. By just being. I know now that I am the creator of my own life. As are we all! We are all being responsible for our own life: our thoughts, emotions, actions and reactions - and our relationships with ourselves and others. It´s all up to me and what I make out of life. How I want to feel and what kind of relationships I want to have. What gives me joy and pleasure. Things I need to make space for and to create what it is that I want from life. Not what I don't want, but what I am actually longing for, and dreaming of.

It is also up to all of us. How we are the creators of our lives. It is only when we all take full responsibility for our choices, our actions and our reactions, that we are able to create what we want. The things we long for in life. The choice is always up to each and every one of us. Like one of my many turning points…do I want to die? Or do I want to live? If I do what I usually do, then I will have the same result as I usually get. If I want something else, something different, then I have to think and do things differently. I have the freedom to make new choices every day. I have, of course, always been the creator of my life, but I didn´t know it before. I didn´t realize how powerful my thoughts were and that my thoughts and feelings about myself created my own imprisonment. I didn't understand it, back then.

In the past I created my own misery and my sufferings with my thoughts, feelings and my actions. By changing, and being responsible for my inner universe over time, I changed my perception of myself and of my life and my reality. I created a new reality. A new life. A life much more aligned with who I actually am. My soul´s purpose. Every day is a new day - a new beginning. You also have the power to create your life aligned with you are and what you want.

This acknowledgement to myself creates a warm, soft tingling shiver that moves through my entire body. And another one. More soft shivers. Like subtle waves coming and going in the vastness of the ocean. Constantly moving like soft waves, ever changing, ever moving. But with a significant difference from eleven years ago. This time I allow the movements, and the thoughts, bodily sensations and my emotions to flow freely without me trying to control them, to suppress them or to change them. No resistance. No worries. No anxiety. No sensible fears. Just flow, one way or another. This is now my new, familiar reality. Warm subtle waves of gentleness and happiness flowing easily, effortlessly and abundantly through my entire being. Feeling genuinely at peace and happy. For no reason at all. For the small, intangible things in life. For the big, important things in life. For my kids. My relationship with myself, my friends and other loved ones. My work feels meaningful and exciting to me. I feel happy for being present in the moment. For just sitting here, sipping my tea. Feeling and experiencing freedom, flow and love in life, inside out.

I close my eyes and let tears of gratitude fall warm and slowly down my cheeks. I feel their warmth, as they are letting go and fall freely from my eyes. That longing of my soul I had so many years ago: "I want to be free. I want to be at peace. I want to be happy. I want to love and to be loved. I want simplicity. I want to live my life more simply. I want to live my life plain." It was my choice, my longing, my journey, and it is still a choice I continue to make every day. I am grateful for that possibility! I am finally here now. Finally.

My long, lonely, struggling, bumpy and winding path
is over.
My search for something else in the outer realm, is
finally in the past.
I don't have to look for anything outside of me
anymore.
I don't have to search for, or chase, happiness, love,
confirmation, peacefulness or stillness.
I don't need anything to fill my "inner emptiness".
My inner black hole is not a black hole anymore.

Nobody needs to rescue me, and I don't need to be rescued.
I don't need to fill my days with activities, strategies or doings.
I don't need to be busy, to escape, to fight, to struggle - I don't need to perform or do anything.
I don't need to prove myself.
I don't need to strive.
I don't need to compare myself.
I am a human being, not a human doing!
That in itself is an amazing, fantastic, wonderful and blessed feeling.
My inner realm, my inner reality has forever changed, transformed.
Transformed into something else. Something new.

Because after all these years I finally found out how to fill myself. Just by being and accepting me, and all of my aspects. My different parts, all that I am. I am now acting from love, lust and joy, rather than from fears and worries. So a transformation from a fear-based perspective to a Love-based perspective. An inner journey from my head, and my thoughts into my Heart.

I am, and have always been, whole – I just didn't see it, nor feel it, back then. I didn't know it.
I feel it now though. In every cell, every part of my being. I just know.
I have no more inner black hole. My black hole is gone. Instead

I find myself being whole. Being filled by myself. I am whole.
I am holy.
We are all whole. We are all connected in wholeness.

If I was to the get the same question as I got when I participated
in the 'Stress Rehabilitation Program' a decade ago: "If you could
describe how you feel about yourself and your life in the metaphor
of a bottle of soda, how is it for you now?" I would answer: "My
soda water is now totally transparent, juicy and flowing, with a
lot of bubbly bubbles in all beautiful shades of colors. And the
glass is less thick, delicate and very beautiful, carved in the most
exquisite pattern."

 *The best journey always brings us home.* 
Author unknown.

Yeah, I made it.
Finally, I am here.
At home, at peace.
In myself, with myself, by myself.
In myself, but now also together with others, my beloved
children, partner, family, friends and fellow human beings.
Feeling so alive and grateful.
Grateful for life.
Thank you!

Relax
Release
Receive

Ullis Karlsson

"Relax-Release-Receive"
are the true essence of Ullis Karlsson Heart centered teachings.

Ullis today, 48 years old, working globally on a mission to create a more connected way of being. With a vision of contributing to a better world for us all to live in.

Thank You

Thank You so much for you taking your time to read this book ♥!

This book is finally coming to an end. A rather big chapter in my life that is coming to an end. A closure of my first 48 years. Something ends and something new, something unwritten begins. Like the "Phoenix", something has to die for something else to rise from the ashes. This part, this behavior, had to die, so something new could be born.

I am now again in a huge transition in my life, both personally and professionally. I don´t know what lies ahead of me, but I do have visions, and dreams, waiting to be fulfilled. Again, I embrace and welcome the mystery of the unknown, with a significant difference. This time I truly feel, I really know, I am being led by my heart. I'm being guided by my soul´s purpose.

I hope some parts of this book will resonate deeply with you. Maybe you have experienced something similar and also found your way through your darkness and made it to the other side? If this book can give you some kind of consolation, hope, or maybe make you curious about your own life, I am very grateful for that. Perhaps your own journey, where you have been and where you are going will become more transparent to you. I also hope that some things might inspire you - even if it´s only one sentence in the whole book. That sentence might create an ignition for you to be able to create the change you are seeking in your own life!

Most of all, I wish that you too can find a way where the longing and calling from your soul is greater than all your accumulated fears. And, that by the end of the day you also choose to follow your heart, no matter how hard it might seem when you take your first step! Just remember, you need to start somewhere, at some point, taking one small step at a time. May you, and your journey be happy and prosperous!

To hear the voice of your Heart, the whisper from your soul you need to be in silence, and you need to be still!

With Love and Light,

Ullis Karlsson
Stockholm, Sweden 2019

www.ulliskarlsson.com

Contact information

If you want to connect with me,
my website is: www.ulliskarlsson.com

Mail address:
ullis@ulliskarlsson.com

Facebook:
https://www.facebook.com/profile.php?id=100000261784102

Instagram:
https://www.instagram.com/ulliskarlssoncom/?hl=sv

For all the readers of this book, I give a 10% discount on my services including consultations, readings or coaching. I would be very happy to guide you into your inner essence, into yourself!

Ullis Karlsson

Ullis Karlsson Professional Bio:

- ✓ Legitimized Physiotherapist (Hälsouniversitet Linköping)
- ✓ Preschool Teacher (Lärarhögskolan Stockholm)
- ✓ Ashtanga and Power Yoga Teacher (Its Yoga Sthlm SATS, E2, World Class)
- ✓ MediYoga - Teacher and Therapist (The Institute for Medical Yoga)
- ✓ HoliYoga/ HoliYoga Hormon – Yoga Teacher (Shanti Yoga och Kultur)
- ✓ Yoga for Children and Adults with special needs – Yoga Teacher (different courses)
- ✓ Instant Transformation Practitioner (Consiousness technologies)
- ✓ Vipassana Meditation Meditation Practitioner (Vipassana center)
- ✓ Dakini Priestess Sexual Healer (Estera Liberation and Empowerment)
- ✓ Soul Realignment Practitioner (Soul Realignment)

2:47 THE JOURNEY HOME TO MY HEART

9 789151 917368